PROVI   START

How government discovered early
childhood

Naomi Eisenstadt

First published in Great Britain in 2011 by

The Policy Press
University of Bristol
Fourth Floor
Beacon House
Queen's Road
Bristol BS8 1QU
UK

Tel +44 (0)117 331 4054
Fax +44 (0)117 331 4093
e-mail tpp-info@bristol.ac.uk
www.policypress.co.uk

North American office:
The Policy Press
c/o The University of Chicago Press
1427 East 60th Street
Chicago, IL 60637, USA
t: +1 773 702 7700
f: +1 773-702-9756
e:sales@press.uchicago.edu
www.press.uchicago.edu

British Library Cataloguing in Publication Data
A catalogue record for this book is available from the British Library.

Library of Congress Cataloging-in-Publication Data
A catalog record for this book has been requested.

ISBN 978 1 84742 729 8 paperback
ISBN 978 1 84742 730 4 hardcover

Cover design by Qube Design Associates, Bristol
Front cover: image kindly supplied by www.istock.com
Printed and bound in Great Britain by Hobbs, Southampton
The Policy Press uses environmentally responsible print partners

FSC
www.fsc.org
MIX
Paper from
responsible sources
FSC® C020438

Contents

Foreword

My involvement with Sure Start has taken me from managing a Trailblazer programme in the Ore Valley in East Sussex, to Sure Start Advisor for two London boroughs, and now to my current post as Children's Centre Locality Manager, covering five centres across 750 square miles of rural North Northumberland.

Before 1997, the providers of early years services were kept going on low levels of funding, short-term allocations and a system that concentrated on the school system, paying little regard to all that went before children were five years old. The practitioners argued that they needed more money for parenting services, a greater emphasis on the needs of the very young and more research into what works and what makes a real difference to outcomes, but went largely unheard.

Early years services had always been underfunded and to a large extent disregarded, with very little emphasis placed on the care of very young children, whether in the family home or in the wide range of care settings that existed in the mid-1990s. In 1997 came the plan for the piloting of Early Excellence centres, provision for young children that combined extended hours of childcare with the quality of early education. Then, in 1998, a review of how government departments could work in a more collaborative way to improve services for young children was announced. The idea of cross-cutting reviews and interdepartmental collaboration seemed a very simple process, but it was one fraught with problems and historic issues of silo working.

There was an early decision by ministers to focus on children under four, an area classed by Norman Glass, the Treasury official in charge of the review, as a *policy-free zone*. There was also a realisation that improved services for the very young might even result in long-term savings for the taxpayer, a very attractive thought in the light of the huge amounts of money spent on ameliorating the effects of child poverty.

During 1999, I was running a scheme called Play link, funded by East Sussex County Council. The idea was simple. We visited every child aged 18 months in a defined geographical area, an area with high levels of child poverty, poor antenatal health and fragmented and patchy children's services. We offered a one-hour home visit per week for one year; we took in play activities, working alongside the primary carer to provide play-based activity and supporting the parent in their vital role as their child's main educator. The service worked with parental strengths, rather than concentrating on any deficits in their caring role, and sought to help them identify their own answers to any concerns around their child's behaviour.

In addition, we provided family drop-ins, adult learning opportunities, outings and trips, plus very simple practical help, with access to debt advice, housing surgeries, community health support and so on. The scheme worked, with some measurable outcomes. It was locally coordinated and locally driven, but, at the time, we spoke of working more closely together, rather than articulating that what we really wanted was more effective service integration. We simply lacked the authority to get the other key services like health and education to work collaboratively.

Most of the local agencies still operated separately – separate budgets, separate training and separate outcomes – and very little thought was given to how much time, money and effort could be saved by more holistic work with children and families led by local intelligence and based on what would really make a difference, rather than what we *thought* families needed.

And then Sure Start arrived. Following a requested visit from a senior civil servant, we were awarded Trailblazer status, one of the first of 60 Sure Start Local Programmes to be set up. The first element of the process was the delivery plan, we had to cost what was available locally to ensure statutory services did not use Sure Start funding to replace core funding. This proved to be an almost impossible task, as very few agencies were able to define how much they spent per locality – lesson one in how difficult it is to define and fund a local service based on actual knowledge rather than assumptions. Somehow we found a way forward, and the plan was duly written and agreed.

The plans for all Trailblazers were slow to come to fruition and the challenge was to provide ministers with the action and change they wanted, whilst at the same time staying true to the idea of being locally led and locally driven with families setting the agenda, and being at the forefront in terms of governance.

Leadership for the centre was crucial. Naomi's clear vision and her grasp of the complexity of the issues faced by Sure Start Local Programmes enabled us all to believe that what was being asked of us was possible. As the programme grew, her advocacy with government and her fearless approach to all difficulties that came our way filled us with admiration, and a growing belief in what we could all achieve.

The Sure Start model changed as government ministers and government thinking changed. Some original Public Service Agreement targets were deleted and new ones were added, especially those around support for parents and carers to enter or re-enter the labour market supported by affordable and accessible childcare.

We were struggling to deliver to the community whose expectations were huge, to the wider and sceptical local agencies who were increasingly jealous of the money allocated to the early programmes, and to the parents and carers who had heard the promises, attended the conferences and now wanted real change at a pace they could see and that could actually make a difference to them and their children.

More changes followed the 2002 spending review: a change of focus, change of impetus and change of direction. The 2002 Childcare Review and its recommendations of a bigger role for local authorities; the need for greater levels of information-sharing following the Laming report on the death of Victoria Climbié; and the shift from funding that could only be spent on Sure Start Local Programmes to mainstream delivery funded through local authorities were all challenging changes for programmes that were still developing, still learning about their own localities and still seeking to deliver cross-cutting, integrated and joined-up services to a growing number of children as the artificial barrier of tightly defined catchment areas providing services to families living in particular neighbourhoods was relaxed.

The early days of Sure Start were in hindsight a hugely enjoyable roller coaster of development and change. The page was blank and we could design the programmes we felt were needed. We listened to local families, put great burdens on parents who offered to sit on Partnership Boards and spent massive amounts of time with architects and builders as we tried to ensure that the bricks and mortar of the programme supported the dream.

Each day was about change and the struggle to remain true to the need for joined-up services for children and families that enabled those families who wanted to work to find in the Sure Start offer all they needed in terms of support: from childcare that was of a high quality and flexible enough to meet all demands, to excellent information, advice and guidance that supported them in the transition to employment.

Another change soon followed, we now had to support all children and parents, ensuring the childcare offer met the needs of all ages. Schools would now have a major role to play through extended services before and after traditional school hours.

A common recurring theme for Sure Start Local Programmes was the provision of services that families enjoyed and those that actually made a difference to children. In my own programme, some families would attend baby massage and pamper sessions, but had to be convinced that taking part in an Early Start session, making storybooks for their children and learning new nursery rhymes would benefit their children in the long term.

A sharper focus on evidenced-based interventions, wider research about what actually worked and clarity about outcomes for children and the implementation of an Ofsted-based inspection regime heralded yet more change. We were now Children's Centres. Many argued that to leave the 'family' out of the name did us no good at all. We all knew that we needed to provide high-quality childcare and early years learning and play sessions to improve outcomes for all children attending the centres, but we also knew that in order to dramatically change outcomes for children in the long term we needed to help parents and carers change the home learning environment – a far harder task.

We have now learned that the best centres somehow must combine a total support package for families that ensures better outcomes for children. This has to be done by providing high-quality services for the adults, especially those who have even more hurdles to overcome in the search for equitable access to services, and an equally comprehensive, well thought-out and closely monitored offer for every child. We have faced a wide variety of challenges: better service integration, collaboration, co-location, pooled budgets. These are phrases we use on a daily basis, but are we making a difference? I am biased, but, yes, I think we are.

Reading this book gave me pause for thought on all we have struggled with at local level over the last 12 years. I am proud to have played a part in the Sure Start story, and delighted that the story is now being told. Working at local level, it was particularly interesting to read about the key debates and rationale for the changes we have made over the years. We do not yet have an ideal system for working with young children, but we have made tremendous progress.

Jan Casson
Children's Centre locality manager, Northumberland

List of abbreviations

CSR	Comprehensive Spending Review
CYPU	Children and Young People's Unit
DfE	Department for Education
DfEE	Department for Education and Employment
DfES	Department for Education and Skills
DH	Department of Health
DWP	Department for Work and Pensions
ECM	Every Child Matters
EEC	Early Excellence Centres
EPPE	Effective Provision of Pre-School Education
EYFS	Early Years Foundation Stage
EYPS	Early Years Professional Status
FSU	Family Service Units
HLE	Home Learning Environment
HMT	Her Majesty's Treasury
MCS	Millennium Cohort Study
NATCEN	National Centre for Social Research
NESS	National Evaluation of Sure Start
NNI	Neighbourhood Nursery Initiative
NPQICL	National Professional Qualification in Integrated Centre Leadership
OFSTED	Office for Standards in Education
PBR	Pre-Budget Report
PMDU	Prime Minister's Delivery Unit
PSA	Public Service Agreement
PSX	Public Service Expenditure Committee
RCT	Randomized Control Trial
SEU	Standards and Effectiveness Unit
SR	Spending Review
SSLP	Sure Start Local Programme

Acknowledgements

A very large number of colleagues and friends have helped me write this book. I had extremely helpful encouragement and advice on whether this was a story worth telling from Polly Toynbee, Kathy Sylva, Sylvia Thomson and Lee Taylor. Jane Waldfogel was particularly helpful in commenting on the early chapters, giving me tips on basic structure that then influenced the rest of the book. Just getting started was extremely daunting and Jane gave exactly the right combination of encouragement and friendly critique in the first few months of writing while I was at the Population Research Centre at Columbia University. Teresa Smith and Tom Smith have read every chapter and, again, gave the helpful balance of critique and encouragement. Helpful comments on the full draft also came from Gillian Pugh, Rob Gifford and Liz Gifford. Edward Melhuish has been very generous with his time and expertise, both in fact-checking the evaluation results and in helping with the understanding of what the results meant. Many others have read particular chapters, advising on the sense of the analysis, fact-checking and sharing memories of key events. Among these were Lucy de Groot, Althea Efunshile, Dorit Braun, Barbara Hearn and Michael Moutrie. Many colleagues still working in the civil service were extremely helpful in ensuring the facts and sequencing of events were accurately recorded. Help on the title and cover design came from Nathan Eisenstadt and Charlotte Randomly.

I am particularly grateful to the former ministers and advisors who generously gave their time and spoke with frankness and honesty when interviewed for this book. It was a privilege to work for these ministers, and I greatly enjoyed having the opportunity to meet with them again and reflect on our shared experience of Sure Start. David Blunkett, Tessa Jowell, Yvette Cooper, Catherine Ashton, Margaret Hodge, Estelle Morris and Beverley Hughes all played critical roles in the Sure Start story and agreed to comment on the record, as did Carey Oppenheim, Robert Hill and Geoff Mulgan. Finally, the Nuffield Foundation generously provided a grant for the expenses incurred while writing the book. While I am grateful to all of the above for their contributions, we all hold varying views on the Sure Start story. Any errors or misjudgements are entirely my own.

How it all start

In the spring of 1998, Norman Glass, a senior civil servant from the Treasury, spent a day visiting two community projects in Birmingham. At the time, Glass was in charge of the Comprehensive Spending Review on Services for Young Children. As part of gathering evidence for the review, he was keen to see how such services actually operated at the front line. I was then Chief Executive of Family Service Units (FSU), a children's charity working with disadvantaged families mainly in inner city areas. FSU had two units in Birmingham, one in Small Heath serving a largely Bangladeshi and Pakistani community and one in Pool Farm, on the south edge of Birmingham, serving a largely low-income white community. I invited Glass to Birmingham to show him how very different communities could be from each other in the same city within a few miles. I organised the visit, so Glass and I rode on the train in a standard class carriage (as FSU was paying for travel, first class would have been entirely inappropriate). This visit, and many more like it all over England, led Glass to recommend the creation of a new programme called Sure Start. It would operate in low-income areas, provide a range of services for young children and their parents, encourage the involvement of local parents in its governance structures and be open to all families with young children in the area. The expected outcome of the programme was a reduction in the disadvantage that low-income children experienced on school entry.

My Sure Start journey began when someone from the Treasury rang me at FSU, and asked that I come into the Treasury to speak to Glass about young children and poverty. As will be described later in this book, a request from civil servants in the Treasury was an entirely new experience for those of us who had been working in the voluntary sector for years on children's policy. I remember having to ask for the address. I particularly remember sitting on a sofa in Glass's office that appeared later that evening on a television documentary about John Major. Apparently it had been Major's sofa when he was Chancellor and Glass had rescued it from the basement of the Treasury building. For an American with a background in early years and childcare work, this was all terribly exciting. I had arrived in the UK some 20 years earlier and worked initially as an assistant in day nurseries before setting up a children's centre in Milton Keynes. Having worked for several years at the front line, and then in management jobs in the voluntary sector, I never anticipated being asked my view about the needs of children by senior civil servants. Furthermore, no government of either main party had shown much interest in early childhood before.

This book tells the story of what happened over the next 12 years in policy and practice for young children following that first meeting with Glass. It tells the story of how a new government decided to invest in young children, what their hopes were for that investment and to what extent those hopes were realised.

The story has three interweaving parts. It is a personal memoir of my Sure Start journey, it tells the story of the enormous growth of services for young children over the last 12 years and it describes how an incoming government developed new ways of making policy. I was in charge of Sure Start and eventually all of early years policy from 1999 to 2006, and have maintained a keen interest in policies concerned with child poverty up to the present time. Entering the civil service at a relatively late age and in a relatively senior position was rather daunting. It turned out that being an American was a huge advantage. I was allowed not to know things, and felt comfortable asking the most basic questions. An additional advantage is accent, in that I cannot easily be put into an identifiable class. Moving from discussions with local residents on low-income estates on what people thought was important, to meetings at the most senior levels of government, was easy for me. I was not perceived as coming from a particular class, nor did I respond with rage or deference to particular accents. However, it took me some time to understand some of the civil service rules. When first asked if I was available to meet with David Blunkett, then Secretary of State at the then Department for Education and Employment, I said 'no', because I had a prior meeting in the north of England. I quickly realised that this was the wrong answer to what was essentially not a question.

This book charts the development of Sure Start from the viewpoint of neither an academic historian, politician nor career civil servant. The analysis, observations and sometimes theories on how and why things happened reflect my own perspective, someone who started out working directly with families and young children. Others may see things differently. My perspective is not through the lens of a particular profession like teaching or social work. Indeed, in Britain in 1996 there was no recognised profession for early childhood and I had already been told that my California Credential in Early Childhood Education was not sufficient training to allow me to teach in nursery schools or classes in England.

2

The story is pretty similar to fictional drama. It starts with tremendous hope, has a middle period of doubt and worry, and ends with optimism for the future while acknowledging the struggles and achievements along the way. As of the early part of 2011, much of what has been achieved for young children during the decade from 1997 onwards has remained in place and has been spared the dreadful cuts necessitated by the financial crisis of 2008. There are ongoing debates about what kind of early years services the nation needs, but no longer arguments about whether the nation needs these services at all. This is a huge achievement in itself. Getting to where we are has been difficult, and sometimes a personally painful and arduous journey. I held many strong beliefs about how services should be delivered to improve the life chances of children that turned out to be unfounded when practice was tested with rigorous evaluation. But my core belief in the importance of the life experiences of children when very young to their future prospects remains unshaken.

The Sure Start story is also a case study of policy development under the New Labour government of 1997. While early years policy was only a very small aspect of what the government hoped to achieve, it illustrates much of how the new government wanted to go about its business. It was about working across traditional departmental and professional boundaries; it was about creating policy from evidence of need and evidence of how most effectively to meet need; and it was a part of Tony Blair's commitment to education reform and Gordon Brown's desire to carve out a social policy role at the Treasury. The story shows the messy nature of policy development. Ministers have strong views and personal relationships can enhance or, indeed, hold up policy development. Nonetheless, the ministers I worked with showed unstinting commitment to improving the life chances of children. Indeed, many of the changes to Sure Start were a result of ministers taking extremely seriously research evidence about what was going well and less well. The programme grew and matured and, along the way, had enormous impact on the radical changes to the management and delivery of services for children across the age range.

As far as possible, I have written in chronological order, but some of the aspects of the story need to be told separately:

- Chapter 2 describes the policymaking context of the New Labour government. It explains the enthusiasm of ministers not only to make new policy, but to change the policymaking process, making it more inclusive of outsiders and based on evidence instead of ideology. It explains what Labour had promised during the 1997 election for young children, and how the early years agenda developed in the first year or two of the New Labour government.

- Chapter 3 describes the Comprehensive Spending Review process and the conclusions of the Review on Services for Young Children. It challenges the presumption that the original design of Sure Start was based on evidence of what works, and describes how an incredibly inclusive process of policy design, engaging outside practitioners, academics and civil servants, led to the distinctive elements of the early Sure Start programme.

- Chapter 4 tells about the struggle to actually get activity happening at local level. It explains why it took so long to get services established, and the understandable impatience of some ministers with the inordinate delays. It then goes on to describe the debate and decision to double the size of Sure Start barely 18 months after its creation.

- Chapter 5 describes the politically charged and arduous process of commissioning the evaluation of Sure Start. It explains why Sure Start was so difficult to evaluate, the arguments about the fundamental design of the programme that made evaluation highly problematic and the storm that erupted when the results of the tendering process were announced.

- Chapter 6 is mainly about the radical changes in children's policy after the 2001 election, and what those changes meant for Sure Start. It describes the new emphasis on child poverty and the links to lone-parent employment that had not been part of the initial Sure Start story. It then goes on to describe how the changes encompassed in the Every Child Matters agenda from 2003 created a drive to move the administration of Sure Start from central government to local authorities.

- Chapter 7 begins with two key changes in Sure Start and ends with the story of the presumed death of Sure Start. This part of the saga involves the integration of Sure Start with mainstream policies on early years and childcare, and then the development of a publication that would shape all early years and childcare policy for the next 10 years. The publication of *Choice for Parents, the Best Start for Children, a Ten Year Strategy for Childcare* became the focal point around which debates played out on whether Sure Start as originally envisioned had a future.

- Chapter 8 gives an extensive summary of the results of the evaluation, and what was learned about key features of Sure Start that were and were not working. It describes a series of reports that attracted significant negative publicity about whether Sure Start would deliver on its early promises, and how ministers responded to the reports, changing the programme in line with the emerging evidence, and held their nerve, continuing to support Sure Start.

- Chapter 9 gives an overview of what has been learned from previous chapters, and what the pointers are for the future of early years and childcare. It acknowledges the disappointment in the failure to reduce inequality, while celebrating the success of a well-established and entrenched infrastructure of services for young children that has been shown to improve outcomes across all groups of children. It then offers some key dilemmas and lessons for the future of policy and practice.

TWO

Setting the scene for change

Two key elements define the context for the establishment of Sure Start: the desire of the New Labour government to develop policy in new ways, including an ambition to reform the civil service, and the genuine commitment of the new government to improve and expand services for children, particularly early years and school provision. Underlying both of these, and critical to the New Labour project, was the unusual relationship between Gordon Brown and Tony Blair. This chapter will describe the wider policy context for Sure Start, and how politics as well as policy and personalities set the stage for radical developments in children's services.

If Gordon Brown and Tony Blair had had the traditional relationship between Chancellor and Prime Minister, there probably would not have been a Sure Start. Children and disadvantage would have been a priority for the new government, and much would have happened, but the particular way in which Sure Start was developed owed much to the increased power in the Treasury on domestic policy issues. The famous *Granita deal*, where Blair promised Brown, as Chancellor of the Exchequer, unprecedented authority on domestic policy issues, gave Treasury officials a chance to design innovative approaches to policymaking almost independently of the government departments that would have to implement the policies they were designing. In part, this was made possible by one of Gordon Brown's first actions as Chancellor of the Exchequer, handing over control of interest rates to the Bank of England. This left a cadre of high-level officials at the Treasury with time on their hands. They used the time to radically redesign the way in which the Treasury allocated taxpayers' money to fund public services (Melhuish and Hall, 2007, p 3).

New ways of making policy: the Comprehensive Spending Review process

A new government was determined to develop policy in new ways, and the Treasury was leading on a new way to set and monitor government spending. Gordon Brown's dominance of the political scene led to a significant increase in power to the Treasury. The Comprehensive

Spending Review (CSR) process was a radical departure from the traditional annual budgetary process. It gave the Treasury not just its traditional role in setting spending limits for government departments, but also a major role in domestic policy more generally. The CSR process gave the Treasury authority to negotiate not just how much money departments would get, but, more importantly, what they were expected to achieve with the money. While most of the CSR negotiations were conducted between the Treasury and individual departments, in keeping with the desire to tackle some issues that involved several different government departments, a small number of cross-cutting reviews were started in 1997. Among these was the Comprehensive Spending Review on Services for Young Children. The CSR process and development of Public Service Agreements will be described in more detail in Chapter Three, but the Treasury's greatly enhanced role was critical to the development of Sure Start.

New ways of making policy: the Modernising Government agenda

Policy innovation was not just coming from the Treasury; the Prime Minister was himself very keen to develop new policies in new ways. The rationale for the innovation in policy development was set out in a White Paper of March 1999, *Modernising Government*. It described the reasoning behind some of the processes that were already well under way since the election, and the core principles that the government would be using to develop policy in the future. The document describes a number of key public services in need of *modernisation*, including: the NHS, the welfare system, the criminal justice system and constitutional reform. The White Paper then goes on to say:

> But modernisation must not stop there. To achieve these goals we must modernise the way government itself works:
>
> * The way we devise our policies and programmes.
> * The way we deliver services to individual citizens and businesses.
> * The way we perform all the other functions of a modern government....
>
> [I]n general too little effort has gone into making sure that policies are devised and delivered in a consistent and effective way across institutional boundaries – for example between different government departments, and between

central and local government.... An increasing separation between policy and delivery has acted as a barrier to involving in policy making those people who are responsible for delivering results in the front line. (HMSO, 1999, p 9)

Key features of the New Labour project emerged in this White Paper: an emphasis on blurring the traditional lines between policymaking and implementation; and a desire to engage at all levels, and to work across Whitehall, breaking down departmental boundaries. Public services were to be user- not provider-led, designed around the best evidence of what works, inclusive, innovative, and driven by clear measurable outcomes, not inputs. Particularly important to this new way of developing policy was a very strong emphasis on the use of research evidence. Indeed, some tensions in the modernising principles were also already emerging. The desire to be user-led and to be based on clear evidence of efficacy, and the desire to be innovative, while basing delivery of new services on clear evidence of what has been shown to work elsewhere; these principles are not mutually exclusive, but they can sometimes be in tension. It was clear that, even this early, Sure Start was seen as a pioneer in this new policy environment. Sure Start is the first boxed example described in the *Modernising Government* White Paper:

Cross-cutting policy in practice – Sure Start

The Comprehensive Spending Review showed that services for children under four years old are patchy and fragmented. Research demonstrates that early intervention and support is important in reducing family breakdown; in strengthening children's readiness for school; and in preventing social exclusion and crime. The aim is to work with parents and children to improve the physical, intellectual, social and emotional development of young children.

Cross departmental groups, involving people with an interest in health, education, the local environment, juvenile crime and family welfare as well as local government and the voluntary sector, were set up to devise and implement Sure Start. They have come up with an initial programme of 60 pilot projects – announced in January – based on evidence of what works and on the principle of learning from those with a track record in delivery. (HMSO, 1999, pp 15–17)

All new governments promise change, and commentators often respond to these pronouncements with some scepticism. But the new ways of working were taken very seriously by the various bodies who audit public expenditure. The audit bodies approached the modernising agenda with attitudes of cooperation as well as concern about what critical issues would need to be considered in this new way of making and delivering policy. What were the inherent risks in joined-up government and in closer working, particularly with pooled budgets and outcome rather than input measures? The promise was for better, more efficient public services that not only would meet the needs of users, but were, at least to some extent, shaped by them. The key challenges in such an approach were documented in a follow-up paper, *Implications for Audit of the Modernising Government Agenda*, published in April 1999 by the Public Audit Forum, a consortium made up of the National Audit Office, the Audit Commission, the Accounts Commission for Scotland and the Northern Ireland Audit Office. The need to break down traditional departmental and professional silo working was a major theme in the modernising agenda. The terms 'silos' or 'silo working' are used in this context to describe highly vertical structures where staff work within a particular discipline like health, education or housing, and do little to make contact or work with other disciplines or organisations. While working in silos may be unhelpful because it often results in end users experiencing fragmented public services, silos are particularly useful for accountability, in both performance management and financial terms. Breaking down silos and more integrated working posed at the time, and continues even now to pose, some serious problems. In its paper, the Public Audit Forum identified six major challenges in the new way of working:

- The need for new forms of accountability
- The readiness of auditors as well as managers to embrace change
- The challenge of assessing value for money where more than one body is involved
- The importance of performance measurement
- The need to maintain financial discipline and ensure the legality of expenditure
- The importance of co-operative working between auditors. (Public Audit Forum, 1999, p 7)

The relevance of these challenges to Sure Start will become clearer in future chapters, particularly in Chapter Three on governance arrangements for Sure Start, Chapter Five on designing the evaluation and Chapter Eight on what the evaluation told us about value for money . For now, it is important to note the irony that the government's efforts to make public services more seamless were creating new ways of working that often increased bureaucratic processes. Two of the issues on the list above were particularly difficult for Sure Start, as well as many other new programmes. Outcomes in early years services can only be measured over a relatively long timescale, and require data-collection systems that in 1997 simply did not exist. Establishing new data-collection systems would prove to be onerous. Second, value for money is complicated when more than one organisation is contributing and, more importantly, when the organisation that will eventually save money may not be the organisation that makes the investment. There was already evidence from the US that high-quality early years services reduced juvenile crime rates, hence saving huge amounts of money on criminal justice services. But these programmes had been running in the US for many years. If this were to be the case in the UK, the savings would accrue to the criminal justice system, not the local authorities making the investment, and would only come some 10 to 15 years after the investment was made. Nevertheless, officials in the Treasury were particularly interested in prevention and early intervention as a means of saving money over the longer term. This argument will be further discussed in Chapter Three.

Modernising the civil service

A key element of the modernising agenda was the reform of the civil service itself. The Cabinet Office Permanent Secretary, Mavis McDonald, chaired a project which identified six key priorities that would be needed to realise the *Modernising Government* agenda. One of the priorities was the need for a programme to modernise the civil service. In 1999, Sir Richard Wilson, then Cabinet Secretary, reported to the Prime Minister on the changes that would be needed in the civil service to ensure that the government's programme would be delivered effectively. Sir Richard suggested that the right changes to the civil service would result in:

- A tougher emphasis on results and outcomes, identifying the root causes of problems particularly for cross cutting areas;

- Better researched, more innovative solutions to problems; a wider range of experience, ideas and professionalism, both from inside and outside the Service;
- A better European focus;
- More creative and collaborative working, actively managing risk;
- Civil servants taking greater pride in what they do. (Cabinet Office, 1999)

Again, a coherent set of themes appears in this list: an emphasis on outcomes and evidence and the use of a broader range of experts. The new element is about civil servants taking pride in their work. One wonders why there is an assumption that civil servants were not proud of their work before 1997. This oblique reference probably deals with what at the time was a thorny issue for ministers and the most senior civil servants. Ministers wanted deep commitment to results and delivery. Civil servants feared a threat to the civil service code built on political impartiality. Was it the job of civil servants to explain new policies or to promote and defend policies? Traditional civil servants found some of this very hard. To reform the civil service required traditional civil servants to change some of their behaviours as well as bringing in a new kind of civil servant, one from the outside who had worked in the relevant policy area. What was learned rather quickly, and sometimes at some cost, was that these new ways of working required both the traditional and highly developed mandarin skills alongside the passion and different kind of energy of experts who often did not have a particular political agenda as much as a deep commitment to making things better for any number of particular groups: children, homeless people, young offenders. It is also true that many civil servants were very enthusiastic about the new ways of working. It was ministers who viewed them, sometimes unfairly, through the prism of the old *Yes Minister* stereotype. This stereotype presented civil servants as resistant to change and immensely powerful in their ability to *stop* things from happening. My early experience in the civil service was different; I worked with highly skilled people who understood the workings of the machine, but often had little experience of the impact of the machine on the wider environment. Basically, civil servants needed to get out more.

The dramatic change for those working outside the civil service was that a small number of very senior jobs were now being openly advertised for non-civil servants. The notion of a generalist policymaker who could develop policy on employment for a year or two and then move on to agriculture was beginning to change. An expert from Shelter, the housing charity, was brought in to run the strategy on reducing rough sleeping. A senior police officer was brought in to develop the drugs strategy. The Social Exclusion Unit, while run by a high-ranking Treasury civil servant, was largely staffed by outsiders. Its work was steered by a broad range of stakeholders from the voluntary sector, local government and academia. It is difficult in retrospect to recreate the excitement of the time. For those of us on the outside of government, who had been spending years trying to influence policy with only limited success, the opportunity to contribute to these groups was fantastic. Hence, it should have been no surprise that when the decision was taken to establish the Sure Start programme, the Head of Unit post was advertised externally. Indeed, in the event, no civil servants even bothered to apply, so strongly was it assumed that the role would be filled by someone from outside the civil service whose primary focus was children and poverty, not generic policy development. Norman Glass phoned me, saying he hoped I would apply for the post. At the time, I was Chief Executive of a children's charity, Family Service Units. Having only been in the post for two-and-a-half years, I did consider not applying for Sure Start, but the temptation was too great.

After a lengthy and challenging recruitment process, I was phoned in November 1999 and asked if I would be willing to meet with ministers Tessa Jowell and Margaret Hodge for a final interview before appointment. Again, given the political impartiality of the civil service, I was told I could refuse to see ministers, and it was not a formal part of the recruitment. Ministers were agreeing (or not) to the proposed candidate, and would have had no other involvement in the recruitment process. Eighteen months after the election victory, New Labour was changing the way policy was developed, engaging a new kind of civil servant to support the changes and implementing a new process for allocating funding to departments. From the start, children were meant to be the intended beneficiaries of these changes.

New Labour and children

The first key element of the context for Sure Start was the desire to make policy in new ways. The second and clearly more important element was the new government's commitment to children, and to tackling disadvantage. There was a lot to do. The previous 30 years had seen considerable policy debate, but very little action on young children from either Conservative or Labour governments. In 1980,

Jerome Bruner published his seminal study of provision for children under five in Britain. His conclusions make salutary reading, reminding us of how far we have come:

> The provision of childcare in Britain since the war is a curious counterpoint of unfulfilled official declarations of intent and voluntary response filling gaps left by inaction. In 1978 Britain had one of the poorest child care records in Western Europe in the maintained sector. (Bruner, 1980, p 32)

Bruner went on to praise the level of voluntary provision in Britain, with mainly mothers delivering significant levels of childcare services for little or no reward. Inevitably this resulted in patchy availability and quality, and rarely suited the needs of working women.

Gillian Pugh, writing 16 years later, acknowledged some progress on early years policy, but argued that there was still a long way to go. In commenting on the Conservative government plan to give parents vouchers with which they could choose the provision they preferred for their young children, she commented on the overall lack of an integrated early years policy.

> Developments over the last decade have created a number of building blocks in an early years policy.... The concern for quality and quality assurance is to be welcomed, as is the emphasis that the Children Act places on co-ordination and review, and on responding to children's cultural and linguistic background. The demand for day care is forging some imaginative partnerships, and the need for further expansion is generally more widely understood. But the introduction of a system of vouchers for the parents of four-year-olds is a diversion that fails to confront the need for a national policy that reflects the areas outlined in this chapter, or the broader issues of work and family responsibility. Fragmentation, lack of resources and lack of vision persist in preventing all children having access to the start in life they so richly deserve. (Pugh, 1996, p 29)

In 1986, Pugh had set up the Early Childhood Unit at the National Children's Bureau, and for years had been an effective and vocal campaigner on early years policy and practice. The key recommendations made in the second edition of *Contemporary Issues in the Early Years* include the need for a clear legislative framework for provision, quality standards, expansion of services and engagement with parents (Pugh, 1996). These same issues are very much reflected in Labour's policy developments in its first term in office. Much had been argued and discussed before 1997. A small group of academics, practitioners and policy campaigners had been active. There were clear links to the feminist movement and the desire for increasing numbers of women to seek employment. However, Labour's policy pronouncements on children came from pragmatic as well as progressive motives.

The Labour commitment to children is most obvious in the pledges on education in the 1997 manifesto. Indeed, Blair's sincere passion about education is evident. But there is also a clear effort in the manifesto to distance New Labour from the 'old' Labour Party of the past. Concentrating on children allows an emphasis on disadvantage without the traditional Labour baggage of class divides. Blair writes in the introduction to the 1997 Labour Party election manifesto:

> In each area of policy a new and distinctive approach has been mapped out, one that differs both from the solutions of the old left and those of the Conservative right. This is why new Labour is new. We believe in the strength of our values, but we recognise also that the policies of 1997 cannot be those of 1947 or 1967. More detailed policy has been produced by us than by any opposition in history. Our direction and destination are clear....
>
> We will be a radical government. But the definition of radicalism will not be that of doctrine, whether of left or right, but of achievement. New Labour is a party of ideas and ideals but not of outdated ideology. (Labour Party, 1997, pp 4–5)

Several of the pledges in the 1997 manifesto are obliquely related to disadvantage, but expressed in language meant to appeal to a wider constituency than the traditional political left and the voluntary-sector lobby groups. Parents will have increased powers, but also increased responsibilities, the clear implication being that some parents do not fulfil their responsibilities. There is considerable space in the manifesto given to youth crime and tackling drug addiction, both highly correlated to disadvantaged groups. The most explicit of the anti-poverty elements of the manifesto are about welfare-to-work policies aimed particularly at young people and at lone parents. Again in the manifesto:

Today the main connection between unemployed lone parents and the state is their benefits. Most lone parents want to work, but are given no help to find it…. Once the youngest child is in the second term of full-time school, lone parents will be offered advice by a proactive Employment Service to develop a package of job search, training and after-school care to help them off benefit. (Labour Party, 1997, p 19)

And not only lone parents, but workless households with children are mentioned:

Families without work are without independence….
    Labour's national childcare strategy will plan provision to match the requirements of the modern labour market, and help parents, especially women, to balance family and working life. (Labour Party, 1997, p 25)

The 1997 Labour manifesto had two commitments concerning young children: the anti-poverty offer was the promise of a national childcare strategy that would enable women's employment; and the offer for all children was free nursery education provision for four-year-olds within the first five years of the new government, and a commitment to setting a target for expanding the offer to three-year-olds. The Conservatives had only very recently set up a nursery voucher scheme that allowed parents a certain number of hours of nursery care to be used in public-, private- or voluntary-sector provision. Local authority provision of nursery education was extremely patchy, with the majority of three-year-olds and a very large portion of four-year-olds getting their early years group experience from voluntary-sector playgroups. The voucher scheme was intended to stimulate a market in nursery provision from which parents could choose. The Labour policy at the time was to close the voucher scheme and use the funding for the expansion of state nursery education provision. At the time, there were three main types of early years provision:

- childcare suitable for working parents usually staffed by people with few if any qualifications, offered full or part time throughout the year. Often childcare was available for children from infancy through age four. Usually parents paid for childcare and it was provided by private, voluntary and public sector organisations. Childcare policy was managed from the *employment* side of the DfEE [Department for Education and Employment], seen as critical to gender equality in employment;

- nursery classes and schools, staffed by a combination of teachers and trained nursery nurses, offering half day care five days a week during school term times for three and four year olds. Nursery classes and school provision was free, provided by the state. Nursery education policy was managed from the *schools* side of the DfEE;

- playgroups largely run by volunteers with a wide variety of training and backgrounds, and usually offering part time term time only, often only two or three mornings a week for three and four year olds. Parents usually paid a very small fee for playgroup places. (Eisenstadt, 1982, p 10)

Early Excellence Centres (EECs) were to lead the way in breaking down the care–education divide in the early years. A further commitment was made in the manifesto to pilot a number of EECs. The distinctive feature of these centres was a flexible offer of day care suitable for working parents combined with the quality inherent in early education.

EECs employed trained teachers as well as less-qualified nursery staff. The rationale was sensible; the needs of the child for a quality experience do not change depending on the needs of the parent for full- or part-time care. A small number of these centres had been around for quite some time, particularly in Islington where they had been established under the political leadership of Margaret Hodge. Some of them offered a much wider range of services, including parent support, outreach and home-visiting for particularly disadvantaged families. EECs also varied in charges for parents, some were totally funded by the local authority and charged no fees, others charged parents for the day care, but not for the wider support services.

While there was evident commitment to early years provision in the 1997 Labour manifesto, the provision had two quite distinct aims: providing all children with early education and providing childcare to support the welfare-to-work policies. There is an absence in the manifesto of two key issues that quickly became of major interest for Labour once in power: service integration, building services around the complex needs of individuals and families rather than particular professional interests; and prevention and early intervention, providing services early enough to prevent problems becoming desperately acute. Indeed, the word *prevention*, so commonly used in relation to the importance of high-quality parent support in the early years, only appears in the manifesto in the section on crime. Integration was not yet used, and in practice is referred to the integration of childcare and early education in the pilot EECs. There was as yet no mention of the wider integration of children's social care, health, parent support and employment advice.

The 1997 manifesto clearly demonstrates New Labour's commitment both to children and to disadvantage. The development of Sure Start within barely two years of the election is not surprising. It was consistent with the need to ensure that any explicitly anti-poverty work was about children, the blameless poor. However, within the manifesto there was a clear separation between policies for all children (ie universal nursery education) and policies about poor children (ie getting lone parents into work). Aside from the modest commitment to pilot EECs, the manifesto describes the nursery education pledge completely separately from expanding childcare, getting lone parents into work or, indeed, supporting families. The *joining up* or service integration agenda was yet to come, and would be a hallmark of the new government. It had not yet found a home in children's services. Sure Start was a major new policy, demonstrating all the new ways of making policy, and a precursor to many of the reforms in children's services that would follow under the Every Child Matters banner. It was the beginning of the struggle to really make services for children and families accessible, effective, integrated and seamless.

There are many examples in this book of personal relationships, friendships and animosities affecting the course of policy. Family relationships count as well. One small example of this is rarely mentioned. In 1997, David Miliband worked as a senior advisor in Number 10 and his brother, Ed Miliband, was a senior advisor at the Treasury. Much is made of the influence of their father Ralph, a famous Marxist academic. However, little is mentioned of their mother, Marion Kozak. All the years I had been working in the voluntary sector on children's issues, Kozak had been an active campaigner on childcare. Both Miliband brothers grew up in a household where arguments for better childcare must have been part of daily life. In my view, Marion Kozak is one of the really unsung heroes of the childcare revolution yet to come.

Tony Blair and Gordon Brown really cared about children. They also cared about getting elected and staying in power. This is not an unreasonable position for a party that had been out of power for 18 years. Policy on early years and childcare, therefore, was fertile ground for what was both a deeply felt commitment and politically expedient for both men.

THREE

A star is born

The Labour government that came to power in May 1997 was deeply committed to changing how government works. This chapter will describe some of the policymaking innovation under New Labour, and how it differed from the past. It is difficult to overemphasise the optimism of the times, both within government on what would be possible, and outside of government on what the new administration would deliver. Those of us on the outside working in the voluntary sector were desperate to influence a new raft of ministers, only a few of whom had served in previous Labour administrations. Most had only been MPs during the long years of Conservative rule. Having little experience of serving in government and little knowledge of how ministers traditionally worked was probably an advantage. Ministers really wanted to do things differently and had no old habits to be broken. Two big innovations were developing, one from the Cabinet Office with strong support from Number 10, and one from the Treasury.

One of the earliest announcements that raised significant interest among social policy analysts and lobby groups was the establishment of the Social Exclusion Unit. Peter Mandelson, at the time Minister without Portfolio, announced the new unit in a Fabian Society lecture in August 1997, barely three months after the election. The intention of the unit was to address issues of deep disadvantage that could only be solved with the efforts of more than one government department. Based in the Cabinet Office, and with strong support from the Prime Minister, the unit demonstrated many of the new ways of working that would be a hallmark of the Labour government. Key features of the new unit were an emphasis on cross-cutting policy development and a dogged determination to be inclusive in policy formulation, not just implementation. The new unit operated largely by bringing in advisors from outside of government and setting up consultative processes that engaged front-line staff, policy experts and academics. The early work of the Social Exclusion Unit was driven by high levels of engagement from the Prime Minister, and racked up some impressive successes: strategies to reduce teen pregnancy and rough sleeping to name just two. But it could also be an irritant to mainstream departments. The Unit was investigating problems for Whitehall departments before they agreed that there was a problem. Often the very tight focus of the problem being addressed meant that it was a marginal issue to a big department and did not fit in with bigger problems and priorities. Often, outside stakeholders felt more involved than departmental civil servants who would need to implement the solutions suggested by the Unit. While Sure Start was based in a main spending department, much of the way in which it was set up, and its early operation, was similar to the Social Exclusion Unit: a cross-government approach with a concentration on a particular group and a focused approach on a relatively neglected policy area, which was developed with a large and active group of outsiders.

Comprehensive Spending Reviews

At the same time, the Treasury was establishing its first Comprehensive Spending Review (CSR). Until 1997, public spending by departments was set annually, and was usually a roll forward from the previous year's budget, what is known as the *baseline*. Arguments were largely about how much in addition to the baseline each department would get or, indeed, sometimes about reducing the baseline. It was not about the total expenditure limit. The CSR was essentially a zero-based budgeting process. Each department had to identify its key priorities, state clearly its intended outcomes and what resources would be required to achieve the outcomes. The Chancellor of the Exchequer would chair a special Public Services Expenditure (PSX) committee that included key ministers to agree the final set of priorities. The Treasury would then set out the spending allocations attached to the priorities in settlement letters to each department. These priorities became expressed as Public Service Agreements (PSAs). A set of numerical targets was attached to each PSA. However, for this first round, the funding was announced in July 1998, and the PSAs and targets came some months after.

The real innovation was that spending plans would run in three-year cycles so that departments would be able to plan their spending and activities over a longer period with considerable flexibility over resources that were not spent at the end of year one or year two. Targets attached to the PSAs were for the three-year period, and departments were meant to set trajectories for progress on each of the targets over the period. However, future spending reviews were not to be every three years, but every two years. The 1998 CSR set the spending for 1999–2002. The final year of this spending period would be 2001/02. The next spending review would be in 2000, setting the spending plans for 2001/02 through to 2003/04. The last year of one spending review was the first year of the next spending review. This had two important implications. First, spending planning came around very quickly indeed. Second, each new review revised the PSA targets. This meant that in the final year of one review, departments would be working to achieve the commitments from that review while establishing the trajectories and getting action moving on the next set of targets. While, for many, the changes in the targets were minor revisions, in some areas completely new targets emerged. The overlap of years and carrying two different sets of targets posed some real difficulties.

The Comprehensive Spending Review: Cross-departmental Review of Provision for Young Children

Both the Prime Minister and the Chancellor were particularly interested in forcing better collaboration between government departments. There was concern that secretaries of state often behaved like barons over their own domain, and that more could be accomplished if ministers and their civil servants from different departments worked together. Similar to the rationale for the establishment of the SEU, Treasury officials thought there would be some merit in conducting some cross-cutting reviews on policy areas that were of concern to more than one department. Among these, there was a review on illegal drugs policy, a review on the criminal justice system and a review on services for young children. It was this review, started in the autumn of 1997 and led by an unconventional and brilliant Treasury civil servant, Norman Glass, which resulted in the invention of Sure Start. At the time, Glass was chief micro-economist at the Treasury. He was fascinated by the economic arguments concerning early intervention; getting it right in the early years, particularly for poor children, could mean huge cost savings to the taxpayer later. Glass successfully convinced the Chancellor of the merits of early years. Geoff Mulgan was a senior advisor at Number 10 at the time. He commented that this way of working was consistent with how Brown wanted the Treasury to work:

> "He [Glass] quite quickly persuaded Gordon Brown and others at the Treasury that this was a good thing to do. It was a very good symbol of the Treasury being a very different kind of institution. They wanted to go in and make the Treasury an activist department, they wanted the Treasury to have a social policy capacity ... investigating what would become Sure Start came alongside tax credits as a perfect

exemplar of Treasury being activist, being slightly Santa
Clausish, doing things having good purposes."

The manifesto commitment on nursery education and the piloting
of Early Excellence Centres (EECs) were well under way in terms
of implementation, and were both the sole responsibility of the
Department for Education and Employment (DfEE). While EECs
involved some service integration – education and childcare – it was
clear that a much wider group of departments had some involvement in
services for young children. Furthermore, the Labour policy emphasis
up to this point had been on children aged around four years, and
through the school years. The review would look at services for children
from conception through to seven years. Glass describes the complexity
of cross-government involvement:

> A steering group of officials was set up to carry out the
> Review. Officials representing eleven different departments
> plus No 10 Policy Unit and the by now established
> Social Exclusion Unit as well as the Women's Unit and
> the Efficiency Unit were all involved. This in itself gives
> some indication of the widespread involvement in services
> for young children and the difficulties of developing
> comprehensive programmes. As well as the obvious
> departments like health (including personal social services)
> and education and employment (including childcare) there
> were also social security (benefits for children and families),
> environment, transport and the regions (urban regeneration
> and housing), home office (policy on the family), the Lord
> Chancellor's department (family law), culture, media and
> sport (children's play) and the Treasury (the money), not
> forgetting the Scots, Welsh, and Northern Irish, each with
> their own subtly different mix of policies. (Glass, 1999,
> p 259)

In addition to the officials group, chaired by Norman Glass, there
was also a Ministerial Steering Group. Again, a radical solution to
the problem of such diverse departmental interests was found. The
Ministerial Group would be chaired by Tessa Jowell, who was then
Minister for Public Health. But she would be chairing in her own right,
not as a departmental minister, and would be supported by Treasury
officials. This was highly unusual at the time, but, in the event, worked
particularly well, not least because Glass and Jowell developed a very

good relationship. The first task of the Ministerial Steering Group was to agree the terms of reference for the review:

- to look at the policies and resources devoted to children aged seven and under, in order to ensure effectiveness in providing preventative action and the necessary support to ensure the development of their full potential throughout their lives;
- to consider whether the multiple causes of social exclusion affecting young children could be more effectively tackled at the family and community level using a more integrated approach to provision;
- to take account of policy developments and initiatives being taken forward in other fora. (Glass, 1999, p 264)

Early on there was a realisation by ministers and officials alike that the key area of focus should be on children under four. In part, this was a pragmatic decision, in that the terms of reference required the review to take account of policy development elsewhere, avoiding overlap and duplication. There was considerable activity on children of primary age, for example, a commitment to cut class sizes and to improve literacy and numeracy teaching, and the universal nursery education offer was a firm commitment for all four-year-olds. But the real advantage of looking at new policies for children under four was that this policy area was, using Glass's wonderful phrase, *a policy-free zone*. No particular department or group of officials owned policy on young children, so it was fertile territory without much competition. This was in sharp contrast to drugs policy, which was highly contested territory between the Home Office and the DH. The very existence of a drugs unit at the Cabinet Office implied failure on drugs policy in the other two departments. The drugs policy unit at the Cabinet Office had considerable difficulties, in part because it was contested policy and in part because the outsiders brought in to run it had difficulty adjusting to the Whitehall machine. A policy-free zone meant that there was little existing machinery to deal with, and was an area of keen interest to ministers with none of the potential political baggage of drugs and crime. Furthermore, as described by Pugh and Bruner earlier in this chapter, no one had failed because no one had done much in the first place.

Working with new partners

In keeping with the government's commitment to new ways of developing policy, not just new policies, Treasury officials went to great efforts to involve a very wide group of interested parties in the review. Glass led a small team including Sally Burlington and Sylvia Thomson. Papers were commissioned from external experts, seminars were held exploring the key debates and, most unusual of all, Treasury officials travelled not only to the US to see programmes already well established, but also, with no less enthusiasm although significantly less romance, to the far reaches of England to see home-grown projects.

Again, for those of us outside government, hosting visits from Treasury officials was a completely new experience. We had spent years trying to convince the DH and the DfEE that investment in early years was critical to child outcomes. We were now meeting a wholly different kind of bureaucrat, one who knew virtually nothing about services for poor children, was extremely keen to learn and had huge influence in deciding how public money should be spent. There was an understandable scepticism on the part of spending departments when dealing with children's advocacy organisations. Most of these organisations were both service delivery as well as advocacy groups, and were virtually always looking for government funding. Strong relationships had been built up between government and children's organisations in the past, particularly in the development of the Children Act 1989. The civil servants working in the DH and Department of Education had heard our arguments for many years, both about policy and about funding for particular organisations or projects. As a group, the voluntary sector was often not particularly adept at distinguishing policy arguments from pleas for more funding. The delivery departments that allocated considerable funding from their own budgets for voluntary-sector provision were understandably tired of these pleas, particularly as the hard evidence for efficacy was then pretty scant. Evidence was scant because it was even harder to get funding for high-quality evaluation than it was to get funding for new services.

Engaging with Treasury officials was different. The irony was that the Treasury officials had exactly the same sceptical attitude when dealing with officials from delivery departments that those departments had in working with voluntary-sector organisations. It was the big spending departments that were always wanting more funding from the Treasury, and were sometimes unable to demonstrate what the funding would achieve for the taxpayer. The Treasury officials seemed to think that voluntary-sector partners were not only the font of all wisdom, but free from any self- or organisational interest. Some voluntary-sector players, like Erica De'Ath from the National Council for Voluntary Childcare Organisations, were seconded into the DfEE to work on the review. Furthermore, the funding for voluntary-sector organisations was infinitesimal compared to the kind of figures Treasury officials were used to dealing with for departmental budgets.

Field visits played a major role in the developing romance between the Treasury and voluntary-sector children's organisations. For the first time, Treasury officials were getting out of Whitehall and were really enjoying themselves. For voluntary-sector providers, big and small charities alike, we were meeting very high-level government officials who were genuinely keen to hear what we had to say, and had access to lots of money.

A perfect storm was brewing: a government keen to do good, a large number of *do-gooders* keen to tell them what to do, an emerging body of evidence about what actually would do good that had real resonance with what people wanted to see happen, and, most importantly, there was cash available. Although the government was committed to the spending constraints that they had inherited from the previous Conservative government, they were willing to commit funding to particular areas. Early years policy was one such area. Certainly, the evidence on the importance of the early years for children's long-term outcomes was, and continues to be, incontrovertible. The design of what should be done with children and families in the early years generated much controversy.

Findings from the review

The findings from the review fell into four parts: what was known about the importance of the early years for the development of young children into productive adults; the scarring impact of poverty on young children; the nature of current services for children under eight; and what was known about interventions and services that seemed to make a difference:

- the earliest years in life were the most important for child development, and very early development was much more vulnerable to environmental influences than had previously been realised;

- multiple disadvantage for young children was a severe and growing problem, with such disadvantage greatly enhancing the chances of social exclusion later in life;
- the quality of service provision for young children and their families varied enormously across localities and districts, with uncoordinated and patchy services being the norm in many areas. Services were particularly dislocated for the under-fours – an age group who tended to get missed out from other Government programmes;
- the provision of a comprehensive community based programme of early intervention and family support which built on existing services could have positive and persistent effects, not only on child and family development, but also help break the cycle of social exclusion and lead to significant long term gain to the Exchequer. (Glass, 1999, p 261)

Treasury officials were most struck with the stark connection between poverty and child outcomes. The key message was that poverty was bad for children. Children growing up in poverty had generally less good outcomes than the wider population. Very young children were particularly badly affected by poverty, and families with young children tended to be poorer. At the same time, the government was found to be spending around £10 billion a year on services for children under seven. The largest proportion of this spend was within the DfEE on children already in school, but the rest was spread across the other nine departments that had participated in the review. The departments involved had never considered collectively what the aims were for the expenditure, which department had responsibility for what or how it all fitted together. The real benefits of a cross-cutting review were beginning to be seen. Across Whitehall, policy on young children was fragmented or non-existent. At local authority level, services for young children were patchy, fragmented and of mixed quality. Some areas had a wealth of services for young children, some areas had virtually none. In very few areas did any of the services for children work well together and, even in those areas with lots of services, quality was often mixed at best.

Finally, the review also took a comprehensive look at all the services that seemed to make a difference, both internationally and in the UK. Many of the services studied were delivered by voluntary-sector organisations. Most of these would have been connected to large and medium-sized national charities, but they had extensive local networks and were strongly rooted in neighbourhoods. Hence, instead of coming up with a blueprint for a single new evidence-based intervention with a manual for implementation, the review suggested a set of key features that were almost always in place in services that seemed to make a difference.

- two-generational: involving parents and children
- non-stigmatising: avoiding labelling 'problem families'
- multifaceted; target a number of factors not just, for example, education or health or 'parenting'
- persistent: lasting long enough to make a real difference
- locally driven: based on consultation and involvement of parents and local communities
- culturally appropriate and sensitive to the needs of children and parents. (Glass, 1999, p 262)

Evidence-based?

Given the emphasis across government, and particularly from the Treasury, on evidence-based policy, in retrospect, this actually looks like an odd list. While the American evidence was robust, it does not lead to the above conclusions about programme design. Starting with the first feature 'two generational'; certainly there was considerable evidence that the strongest programmes from the US did work with both parents and children. Particularly admired was the High Scope Program implemented at the Perry Pre-School in a very deprived suburb of Detroit. However, that is where the similarities end. 'Stigma' did not seem to be a concern for High Scope. It was highly targeted on very poor children, and, indeed, Head Start to this day has very high entry barriers based on family poverty (Waldfogel, 2006, p 102). 'Multifaceted' does not stand up either. The High Scope project was originally intended to improve educational outcomes, not to be multifaceted. Indeed, it was many years later that the other benefits started to outweigh the educational gains: better rates of staying on at secondary school, fewer teen pregnancies, less youth crime (Schweinhart and Weikart, 1993). The social outcomes were much more evident than educational gains, and resulted in much of the cost savings attributed to High Scope. Cost savings were made through a reduction in crime, so savings on prison, and higher employment rates and therefore a reduction in welfare dependency.

The inclusion of 'persistence' was intended to set a principle about funding. Many of the apparently effective interventions studied had been funded for one or two years, not long enough to demonstrate any real impact. Provider agencies spent huge amounts of energy looking for money to keep programmes going and found it even harder to find funding for long-term evaluation studies. But persistence was an important operating principle for family support. Given the nature of the design of Sure Start, persistence in the style of family support envisioned beyond the under-fives would prove extremely difficult. This would require schools engaging in family support, which was pretty unlikely at the time.

'Locally driven' is also questionable since, in the first instance, most of the US programmes studied were only in one location and, when disseminated elsewhere, were highly manualised. Progamme fidelity was required, and local variation was strongly discouraged. The evaluations *proved* that a certain set of activities produced good outcomes. Changing the activities through programme variation would risk reproduction of the positive outcomes.

However, 'locally driven' may have come from another innovative service development that was happening in the US and, in a variety of forms, in the UK. Indeed, it may also answer the question of 'multifaceted'. Jane Waldfogel wrote in 1997 about service integration not as a particular intervention, but as an organising principle for services. Service integration was seen to be particularly beneficial for families with complex problems, where one agency would clearly not be able to provide the range of services that might be required. The principles behind local service integration were better delivery for the service user who would not have to navigate a complex web of service entry points, and greater efficiency because there would be less duplication of activities by different agencies with the same family, and better matching of users and their needs (Waldfogel, 1997, pp 467–8).

In the UK, service integration had been tried in a variety of circumstances. Family Centres provided a range of community support services for families with young children from one base, often including part-time group care for young children, parent support, social services, benefits advice and so on. Some offered youth work provision and out-of-school childcare for children over five (Eisenstadt, 1983). The EECs also were providing service integration, although the key feature in these centres was the bringing together of childcare and education. However, many of these also offered the wider Family Centre mix. Some local authorities had tried integration at neighbourhood level, where multi-professional teams, including social workers, benefits advisors and housing support workers, were co-located in neighbourhood offices, rather than town halls. There was long-standing experience of service integration both in the US and the UK, but little hard evidence of efficacy. Service integration was not seen as an evidence-based intervention that had been subject to rigorous evaluation. It was seen as an organising principle that seemed to make sense.

It was found that service integration only worked effectively if it was planned at the local level with both good data on what the population needs were, and extensive consultation to ensure the style of delivery would be appropriate. Both these features relate back to the *Modernising Government* agenda. They are essentially about user-crafted services based on good local data. These both became guiding features for future Sure Start programme planning.

The final required characteristic listed above on 'cultural appropriateness and sensitivity' clearly makes sense. It would be hard to argue that a programme could be culturally *in*appropriate and *in*sensitive to user needs, and still deliver good outcomes. It is also hard to see how this particular feature would have been backed up by any version of rigorous evaluation.

Returning to the discussion in Chapter Two on the *Modernising Government* agenda, some of the core design principles of Sure Start were more to do with what the government wanted public services to be like – close to the user, flexible, user- not provider-led – and not really based on evidence of interventions that had been tested through scientific methodologies. A key aim of the government was to break down traditional silos; the emphasis on service integration at neighbourhood level reflected this aim. They also chimed with what children's campaigners were saying at the time. Indeed, at one conference when Norman Glass was explaining what outcomes the government expected from the newly announced Sure Start programme, I specifically asked him how he could claim that the programme was to be locally driven if the Treasury had already determined what it was meant to achieve. Of course, the review took submissions from a wide variety of stakeholders, and many of these submissions would have argued that the above features were absolutely critical to success. Given the romance connected to voluntary-sector campaigners, it is not surprising that these submissions were accepted as 'expert evidence'. After all, we were running the wonderful programmes that Treasury civil servants were visiting. On these visits, reasonably well-heeled officials were visiting very deprived parts of the country and meeting almost always mothers who were wildly positive about the services they were getting from grassroots organisations. There would have been no way of knowing who was not there, and therefore what proportion of the local population who could benefit from the services were not using them. Nor was there any hard evidence from the UK about their effectiveness in terms of better outcomes for children.

There was no doubt that the evidence on the effects of poverty on children was sound; there was no doubt that the evidence on the poor-quality, patchy quantity and fragmented nature of current provision was sound. The evidence on what the programme should look like was less sound, but nonetheless convincing to officials and ministers. The academics advising the government consistently argued for a more experimental approach: clear standardised inputs that could be tested through rigorous, scientifically accepted methodologies. But there was simply no enthusiasm among ministers, or indeed stakeholders other than the academics, for the programme design to be constrained by what seemed at the time to be highly technical methodological arguments on pinheads. Chapter Five will describe in more detail some of the fierce debates concerning both programme design and evaluation. The design that emerged had features reflecting the incredible diversity of interests that were represented in the review itself. They also reflected the particular passions of the ministers involved at the time: community development, user control, parental engagement and so on. Sure Start became a heady mix of politics, policy and evidence. Most policies are made with selected evidence from different countries and reflect the values and politics of the times. When interviewed for this book in 2010, David Blunkett still held his passion for Sure Start and what he believed it could do for communities:

> "When Tessa Jowell and I talked about it in opposition, we were coming from it in terms of two elements: one was how do you build functioning families, and as a corollary, how do you not only build functioning and civilised communities, but how do you make the two interchange so that the community becomes the contributor, so it builds social capital, so there's capacity and capability of deeply deprived communities to bring out the best in people."

Tessa Jowell, when interviewed, also emphasised the support that women could give each other, but her main aim was about the intimate relationship between mothers and babies:

> "Sure Start started, was really born, in opposition through my experience of my utterly outstanding health visitor and

my Wednesday afternoons at the child welfare clinic at the Kentish Town Health Centre, where I sat for an hour and a half with mums from a whole range of backgrounds. We were united by the fact we had tiny babies, and that some of us were coping less well than some of the others, but the absolutely fundamental point of unity was we could learn from each other and we derived a sense of support and comfort from these sessions we had together.

I started the work on the review [on services for young children] for Gordon and for the Treasury with a pretty fixed view in my mind, which is that what you need when you have a new baby is nurture, and what you need to be able to give your baby is nurture, and you need to have enough confidence to be your baby's first teacher."

Jowell and Blunkett both had worked together on ideas about a Sure Start-type programme. They were particularly influenced by and impressed with the work of Home Start, a voluntary organisation that provided trained volunteers to visit mothers with very young children at home. The key to Home Start was practical support and friendship for women who were sometimes very isolated in the first few years of motherhood.

Margaret Hodge was responsible for the commitment to universal free nursery education in the Labour Party manifesto of 1997. She had also been thinking about a new system of services for young children, but her vision was different again:

"When I wrote the paper before the election, the earliest paper, it was focused on other objectives and it was more about providing, with the child at the heart, an integrated series of services around the needs of that child; part of which was the support necessary for bonding and nurturing, but also it was the early education services."

Sure Start is born

The Sure Start programme was announced in Parliament in July 1998. An allocation of £450 million was made for the first three years, from April 1999 to 2001, to fund 250 Sure Start Local Programmes (SSLPs). For those of us in the voluntary sector, this was an unimaginable sum of money. For the DH and the DfEE, who would jointly run the programme, it was a relatively small sum in relation to their budgets, but it was completely new money. It did not have to be found from existing budgets, so was warmly welcomed. Sure Start was one of many initiatives that poured resources into local areas: for example, New Deal for Communities, Education Action Zones, Health Action Zones and others. As most of these were geographically targeted at poor areas, making sense of the number of initiatives that could be developed in one neighbourhood was challenging.

In December 1998, the aim and objectives for Sure Start were set out by the Chief Secretary to the Treasury within a broader statement about PSAs. This first statement for Sure Start was an interim PSA, to be refined and formalised in the March of 1999. It set out the aim and objectives of Sure Start:

> To work with parents and children to promote the physical, intellectual and social development of pre-school children – particularly those who are disadvantaged – to ensure they are ready to thrive when they get to school.
>
> Sure Start programmes will work efficiently and effectively to achieve this in areas of significant unmet need by:
>
> 1. Improving social and emotional development
> In particular, by supporting bonding between parents and children, family functioning and through early identification and support of children with emotional and behavioural difficulties.
>
> 2. Improving health
> In particular, by supporting parents in caring for their children and promoting health development.
>
> 3. Improving the ability to learn
> In particular, by encouraging stimulating and enjoyable play, improving language skills and through early identification and support of children with learning difficulties. (HMT, 1998a, p 155)

This was a new and innovative approach to local service delivery with some critical key features: programme areas would be selected on the basis of poverty indicators, and all children under four in the area would be eligible to use the services. The assumption was that if the 20% of poorest wards in England were chosen, it would cover about a third of all poor children under four in England. A single programme would be very local indeed, what was referred to as *pram-pushing distance*, covering around 800 children under four. Unlike many other programmes, there was no competitive tendering for funding. It was strongly felt that competitive tenders would further advantage those areas that already had good service leaders who could put together proposals. We intentionally wanted to ensure that poor children were not further disadvantaged by inadequate capacity and leadership at local level.

Developing Sure Start Local Programme plans

In January 1999, Tessa Jowell announced the first 60 areas invited to develop a Sure Start programme. These were to be the 'trailblazers', and much would be learned from these pilots. The chief executive of the unitary council or district council was the initial contact. At district level, a decision would be made on which were the very poorest wards that would benefit the most from a Sure Start programme. This would become the Sure Start Local Programme (SSLP) catchment area. An appointed person would then lead the development of the programme, having to liaise with most of the key services, which were managed at shire, not district, level. Hence, some top-tier authorities like Kent had more than one trailblazer, while large unitary authorities like Sheffield or Manchester would only get one trailblazer in this first round.

Each Sure Start area was required to set up a Partnership Board to oversee the planning. The Board would have representation from all key statutory services, as well as any voluntary-sector providers in the area and, most importantly, local parents. The Board would identify a 'lead body' to be the key contact organisation for all partners and an 'accountable body' to handle the finance for the development of the programme. From the very beginning, David Blunkett held the view that the lead body should not be the local authority. Ministers were very keen that the lead body role be played by voluntary-sector organisations. In the event, while lead and accountable body roles were sometimes taken by voluntary-sector organisations, or by the NHS, the vast majority were local authorities. A very few SSLPs set themselves up as independent charities. While this was consistent with the aims of the community development approach, it was also costly. There were clear efficiencies in having public-sector organisations, or indeed very large charities, as accountable bodies. They could use existing back office services: finance, personnel, planning and so on. I was most anxious to ensure that 250 SSLPs would not mean 500 finance officers and 250 human resources staff. Back office expertise in local neighbourhoods was understandably in short supply, not to mention the skills needed to spend the capital.

The Board was given guidance as to how to develop a plan, and given support if the plan was not good enough. Each plan had to identify what services for young children already existed in the locality, what the gaps were and how the gaps would be filled. There was also a requirement to identify the current spend on very young children to ensure that any new funding would be additive and not replace existing resources from local government, the NHS or charitable trusts and foundations. Civil servants were surprised at how difficult it turned out to be to identify spend on young children. The NHS and local government simply did not account for spend by particular populations. GPs would not know what percentage of their time was spent on families with children under four. Very few services were exclusively aimed at this group, and very many services were connected with them, as well as older children and adults: health visitors, speech therapists, social workers and so on. The nature of the areas also made resource identification difficult. The Sure Start areas were very small, perhaps one or two wards, and sometimes crossing ward boundaries. Administrative data did not exist at neighbourhood level, and most services covered a geographical area much wider than the Sure Start catchment. Hence, identifying specific resources dedicated to particular services, children under four or even the area itself was very difficult.

There was a great emphasis in plan development on consulting with local parents. Local Boards exploited a range of techniques to ensure parents were consulted from open fun days to commissioning the Mori polling organisation to find out what local parents thought was most important. It proved understandably difficult to get parents on the Boards before programmes were actually running, but many areas used existing services to recruit parents to help in the design of their SSLP.

Each programme would need to ensure a set of core services was available locally, either by improving integration of existing services or developing new provision. The key feature was that the services would work as a whole, not as separate offers from different agencies. Rob Smith, a senior official at the DfEE, commented that we were either offering glue in order to bring things together or poly filler in order to fill gaps, the second being considerably more expensive than the first. In fact, we were doing both, but in different configurations depending on local area existing service patterns. The core services required for each programme were:

- Outreach services and home visiting building on existing services
- Support for families and parents, including befriending and social support such as mentoring and parenting information
- Services to support good quality play, learning and childcare for children
- Primary and community healthcare and advice about child health and development and parental health
- Support for those with special needs, including support in getting access to specialised services. (DfEE, 1999, p 4)

Local areas were free to supplement programmes with other services. In keeping with the innovative nature of Sure Start, the programme had its own PSA and related targets. These were published early in March 1999. The key principle here, again looking back on the major innovations of the CSR process, was that the centre of government would define certain outcomes in exchange for freedom to innovate on the inputs that would achieve the outcomes. This important notion of *tight–loose* design was another reason for the resistance to a standardised input model. We wanted to test out if there were different strategies that could be invented at local level to achieve the outcomes. The outcomes were the same for all programmes, but there was a view that because local areas varied so much, not only in their current service models, but also in the nature of the local population, it would be unwise to require a standard input model. We were setting up a very large programme. Being clear on what it was meant to achieve while not being prescriptive on how to achieve it reduced the risks of all the programmes doing the wrong thing. The idea was that programmes would learn from each other. Those that were doing well on the PSA targets would share their strategies with those that were struggling. Two new objectives were added after the publication of the interim Sure Start PSA in December 1998. The PSA targets were a mix of input, output and outcome measures, set out with their objectives as follows:

Improving social and emotional development (objective 1)
- Parenting support and information available for all parents;
- 10 per cent reduction in children re-registered on a child protection register;
- All local Sure Start programmes to have agreed and implemented, in a culturally sensitive way, ways of

identifying, caring for and supporting mothers with post natal depression.

Improving health (objective 2)
- 5* per cent reduction in the proportion of low birth weight;
- 10* per cent reductions in children admitted to hospital as an emergency during their first year of life with gastroenteritis, a respiratory infection, or a severe injury.

Improving the ability to learn (objective 3)
- At least 90 per cent of children with normal speech and language development at 18 months and 3 years;
- 100 per cent of children in sure Start areas to have access to good quality play and early learning opportunities, helping progress towards desirable learning outcomes (early learning goals) when they get to school.

Strengthening families and communities (objective 4)
- 75 per cent of families report personal evidence of an improvement in the quality of services providing family support;
- All local programmes to have parent representation on local programme boards.

Increasing productivity of operations (objective 5)
- At least 250 local programmes in England;
- 100 per cent of families in contact with local Sure Start programme within the first two months after birth;
- Evaluation strategy in place by 2000–01. (HMT, 1999, p 11)

* Target to be reviewed

While there were some clear benefits to this new way of working, the total number of PSA targets proved unmanageable. Hence, each successive CSR attempted to reduce the number of PSAs and associated targets across government. In 1999, there were some 600 PSAs across government. By 2007, the number had been reduced to 30.

A good plan would include detailed data about the catchment area: how many children and the ethnic make-up of local children; what services existed and the extent to which they were already integrated, or could be encouraged to do so; what gaps there were in the core offer of services; and how the combination of existing and current services would achieve the PSA targets. Given the nature of the early years workforce, this was considerably demanding work, and many areas needed intense support.

In the first round of 60 trailblazer programmes, areas were invited to bid for up to £1 million per year for three years' revenue and around £1 million for capital to establish one SSLP. It was important to emphasise that the funding was not dependent on meeting the targets. This was a new and experimental programme. It was critically important that SSLP managers and staff not massage or manipulate data out of fear of failure. We wanted the sharing of both success and failure in order to learn from both.

Just as civil servants were surprised at the difficulty of establishing local spend on young children, there was a touchingly naive view held by Treasury officials that SSLP planners would carry out a rational costing exercise. What do our local parents and children need and want? What is already in place? What will it cost to supplement the gaps and knit together the existing services? And, therefore, how much money do we need? Not surprisingly, almost every one of the first 60 plans came up with a figure very close to £1 million a year for three years.

Only one local authority found it impossible to agree on one area for its programme, so they submitted two plans. Unfortunately, the local area was Sheffield and one of the plans was within the constituency of David Blunkett, then Secretary of State for Education and Employment, and the cabinet minister responsible for Sure Start. He saw no reason, given the level of need in Sheffield, that they should not have two programmes in the first round. This was my baptism of fire as a newly appointed official, and demonstrates how important the mix is between high-level civil servant process skills and outsiders who just want to get things moving. As officials from Sheffield had written to me about their submission for two programmes, I had no compunction about writing back to explain that in the first round, it was one programme per area, and the area itself should decide which one. I had no idea that protocol required me to clear such communication with the Secretary of State, as it was his constituency. David Blunkett was not pleased, but as an official, I also had a duty to protect him for what could be seen as personal interference in a process to allocate resources. Hence, I wrote to him emphasising that the guidance had gone out to all 60 areas and the dangers in making an exception for Sheffield.

The conflict was resolved by ensuring that Tessa Jowell, who led on Sure Start from the DH, decided on which area would go ahead in this first round. Given that our target was 250 programmes, there was no doubt that Sheffield would get additional programmes in the future. The first programme was indeed in Blunkett's constituency, and a few months later, on a windy wet August day, we both attended the grand opening on a field in Sheffield. Blunkett was so pleased to see an official attending a local event on a miserable day in August that he forgave me for writing to Sheffield myself. I had the great chance of watching a consummate politician on his local patch, as an MP, not a cabinet minister. Neither of us knew that the other would be there, which made it more fun for me. I spent most of the time talking to local people, not hanging on to *my* secretary of state. It was a terrific day, confirming my view of the importance of officials actually visiting and talking to local people about what they thought was important.

Innovation in governance arrangements

As officials were getting under way developing SSLP guidance there was recognition of the crucial role stakeholders had played in the CSR and the initial development of Sure Start. So it was decided to maintain two groups to continue advising the fledgling Sure Start Unit: one group made up of general stakeholders who had been involved all along, which came to be known as the *Friends of Sure Start*, and a separate group of academics, who had also been involved, but would be particularly important in advising on the design and then the oversight of the evaluation.

The final piece of the architecture was probably the most radical of all. The overall governance of cross-government programmes was particularly problematic given the conventions of parliamentary democracy. There continued to be a group of officials from across government who would steer the programme. They represented all the interested departments, and the group was chaired by Norman Glass. The unit would be based in the DfEE, although some key external stakeholders argued strongly at the time that it should be based in the Cabinet Office. Their view was that it would be impossible to be both really cross-departmental and operate from a big spending department. The counter-argument, which fortunately won the day, was that the Cabinet Office was not well suited to running spending programmes. It was true, however, that some officials in the DfEE were not comfortable with cross-cutting work, and were particularly uncomfortable with the role of the Treasury in setting policy. It was suggested early on that, as Head of the Sure Start Unit, I should chair the officials group, not Norman Glass. This was expressed as, '*put the Treasury back in its box*'. Like many of the new ministers, I was completely new to government and had no idea what normal relations between the Treasury and spending departments had been like in the past. But I had a voluntary-sector instinct for being excessively polite to those who held the purse strings. Hence, my own view was to hold on to Glass as a valuable patron for as long as possible. Indeed, the line management arrangements were reflective of the cross-departmental nature of the Sure Start Unit. I reported to senior civil servants from the DfEE, the Treasury and the DH. As Head of the Sure Start Unit, I would be an *additional accounting officer* for Sure Start resources, which would be part of DfEE expenditure limits, but strictly ring-fenced for Sure Start purposes.

While the unit was based in the DfEE, the lead minister for day-to-day decisions was to be Tessa Jowell, the Minister for Public Health, who chaired the original CSR and was deeply committed to the policy. The cabinet-level minister would be David Blunkett, then Secretary of State for Education and Employment. Blunkett was also deeply committed to Sure Start, but saw it almost entirely separate from his other early years responsibilities: nursery education and childcare. Hence, while integrating across two departments, a new fragmentation was emerging in the DfEE. Margaret Hodge, the DfEE minister in charge of nursery education and childcare, sat on the Sure Start Ministerial Steering Group, chaired by Tessa Jowell, and was understandably keen on closer working between Sure Start, childcare and early education. David Blunkett seemed to want to keep the areas separate. In the interview for this book, Blunkett still held to the view that keeping Sure Start separate from other early years policy was essential:

> "I wanted it to have a distinct identity. I wanted it to be a programme in its own right that would of course relate to early years because there would be an overlap ... I was concerned that it didn't become an early years childcare operation and that's where the tensions lay. Maybe we were not explicit enough from the beginning in laying out what it was all about, that this was a capacity-building and social capital programme which was going to transform the lives of families and communities, and not just looking after small children."

As an official, this put me in the unenviable position of trying to keep both the Secretary of State and the Minister of State happy in the same department when they essential wanted different things.

Across the DH and DfEE there were also some odd problems of parliamentary protocol in having two ministers from different departments running the programme. Who would answer any parliamentary questions? It was agreed that if there were questions in Parliament on Sure Start, they would be raised in DfEE question time, but answered by a Health Minister, Tessa Jowell.

While this unusual parliamentary arrangement was enormously exciting to traditional officials, I was unsure at the time whether it would make any difference to children living in poverty. Indeed, in reflecting back on the period, I was virtually unaware of how radical Sure Start was, from the local planning flexibilities to the need to agree a different protocol for parliamentary questions. I saw everything through the lens of how I thought it might work for children and families. That is precisely what made me a new kind of civil servant. But Sure Start also needed the traditional kind of civil servant, who knows to check if something is permissible under the law before announcing it and who is aware of what needs to go to ministers for approval and what can be handled at official level. The best civil servants are extremely adept at getting processes to expedite the policies determined by ministers. We needed civil servants from all the different departments we were working with, and from local government and the voluntary sector, our key partners. Most importantly, we needed a team not afraid to ask questions, because none of us had the breadth of knowledge and skills to get this new programme off and running. It was truly a collective effort across central and local government, the voluntary sector, and families themselves.

Expectations for the new programme ran very high. Malcolm Dean wrote a clear and accurate description of Sure Start in a leader piece in *The Guardian* in December 1999. He ended his article with a prediction that set the bar for success very high indeed: 'Just as the Open University was Harold Wilson's proudest achievement, Sure Start could be Tony Blair's' (Dean, 1999, p 17).

The next chapter will describe some of the challenges in making the dream of Sure Start a reality on the ground, while key figures were already moving on to other roles. As will be described later on in this book, setting up and running an SSLP, let alone commissioning major capital works, turned out to be much harder than we anticipated. Ministerial enthusiasm remained undaunted.

FOUR

What happened next?

The next phase of the Sure Start story comes in four interconnecting parts: getting programmes established on the ground; dealing with a change of ministers; the next Comprehensive Spending Review (CSR); and setting up the evaluation. All of these were to have profound effects on Sure Start. The first 60 trailblazer areas were announced in 1999; hence, the most important job from 1999 to 2002 was getting 250 Sure Start Local Programmes (SSLPs) established, spending money and delivering Sure Start in local areas. At the same time, the wider business of government continued. The first reshuffle of government ministers took place in October 1999, and work was starting on the 2000 CSR. It seemed odd even at the time, and even stranger in retrospect, that while we were struggling to get our initial allocation of funding out the door, and had not yet even commissioned the evaluation, we were required to make recommendations to ministers about the programme budget for 2001–04.

Commissioning of the evaluation was also highly fraught. Indeed, the evaluation story is complex enough to warrant two chapters: Chapter Five on how it was commissioned and Chapter Eight on the results.

Getting going: local delivery

The first and probably most important task was to get 250 SSLPs up and running. Ministers wanted visible change on the ground, and civil servants were tasked with setting up a complex approvals process that would put significant amounts of public money into the hands of sometimes local groups that had little or no experience in setting up new services with funding direct from the centre of government. It is no wonder that the civil servants were more comfortable in dealing with a local authority, or at least a major charity, as the accountable body for SSLPs. Ministers, on the other hand, were very clear that they wanted very high levels of community engagement in the planning and running of the new programmes. There was a tension between spending large amounts of public money fast and ensuring local people had a substantial role to play. Other government programmes like the New Deal for Communities were facing very similar challenges. Given the findings of the CSR about the patchy nature of early years services, it is not surprising that both devising and implementing local plans was taking much longer than expected. The desire to bypass the existing infrastructure of local government certainly slowed the process. But it also probably resulted in much more innovation, variety and direct user involvement in local delivery. This is clearly an important message in the current debates about localism. Engaging local people in decision-making can result in more suitable and acceptable services, but it also takes more time.

The antipathy towards local government can be explained in two ways. First, it goes back to the creation of New Labour. Much of what was seen by senior Labour figures as wrong about *old* Labour was played out in local government. There was a concern that handing over this exciting initiative to local authorities would result in *provider capture*. That is, local authorities would use the funding to increase their own staff and do more of what they had always done. Furthermore, it was believed by many in Westminster that what local authorities had done in the past was in large part to blame for making Labour unelectable for 18 years. Second, there was a belief across Whitehall at the time that the best innovation and community traction would come from the voluntary sector, particularly small local groups. This belief is re-emerging currently with the Coalition's desire for Big Society solutions that rely on local activists. Traditionally, policy development control from Whitehall was intended for standardisation, ensuring everyone did the same thing. In the case of Sure Start, it was the opposite; there was a belief that by bypassing local government and promoting decision-making much closer to the user, there would be more innovation at local level, and the match between user needs and appropriate services would be better. However, there was little acknowledgement, and probably little understanding, of how long such processes take. Spending money, particularly in an area of social policy that had never been properly resourced, turned out to be very hard.

Local delivery, as explained earlier, was not easy, so visible change on the ground was limited. The development of plans was taking local areas around 10 months, and even once plans were approved, it took time to recruit staff, find premises and, in many cases, build buildings. The spending was inordinately slow, which meant that the delivery of new services was delayed. In addition, SSLPs that were using their local authority as the accountable body were incredibly slow at reclaiming the money. So, even in areas where spend was happening, the money was still in DfEE accounts. The year one budget for Sure Start was £80 million. We managed to get £5 million spent.

The slow spend was another example of the huge differences in custom and practice between the voluntary and state sectors. I was not aware for several months that not spending the money fast enough was a problem. In the voluntary sector, unspent revenue became part of reserves for leaner times ahead. In the state sector, it is money sitting in accounts that could be put to good use somewhere else, and therefore should be spent. The real lesson is how completely unrealistic we were in expecting the programmes to spend revenue and capital so quickly.

Rob Smith, a senior official in the Department for Education and Employment (DfEE), came up with an excellent suggestion to speed up spend and meet ministers' desire for visible change. He proposed an advance capital grant of £50,000 once an area had been selected, but before plan approval, to support planning. The idea was to have some visible evidence that this particular area was selected for an SSLP. It could be new signage or a play bus in a community setting or a tidied up local park. Ministers could visit and there would be something to see. In the event, the money was not spent to ensure there was a backdrop for photo opportunities for visiting ministers. It was spent on quick wins in neighbourhoods. It was not only ministers who wanted quick and visible change; local people did too. The effect of the early capital investment was to engage people while consultation was happening. Normally, government would consult, go away and consider, and then come back and do something after the residents they had consulted had forgotten that they had been asked their views. This early capital meant that people could see change happening while they were talking about what change they wanted. It had a galvanising effect. One of the most creative ideas was the offer of front fencing for families in the catchment area to ensure that their children could safely play in the front garden. Local people knew we were serious about making things happen. Given that one of the suggested targets for the Public Service Agreement (PSA) was specifically about emergency admissions to hospital, the fences matched what parents wanted and what the programme was meant to achieve. One of the biggest challenges was the alignment of community development methods with positive outcomes for children. Fences preventing children from wandering into the road did both simultaneously. In the Telford example below it was done sequentially; community engagement was first, and activities to promote good outcomes for children were done next.

The early capital project on a Gypsy and Traveller site in Telford also demonstrated community consultation with a service that would result in better longer-term outcomes for children. The site itself was very well maintained by the Telford and Wrekin Authority. But, as with many such sites, it was remotely located with very little easy access to local shops or services. The mothers were consulted on what they wanted from Sure Start. They asked for a children's playground at the back of the site because there was no easily accessible safe place for their children to play. Dylan Harrison, the local Sure Start programme manager, provided the women with catalogues of outdoor play equipment. Together, they came to an agreement on what would work. The chosen equipment had to be within the budget, and Harrison advised on what would be easy to maintain. There was even a question as to whether it was alright to have equipment that might be used by children over four, as Sure Start was for children up to the age of four. The answer, of course, was 'Yes'. The play area was built within three months and the opening was attended by several senior officials from the local authority, including the Director of Social Services, John Coughlan, and the Chief Education Officer, Christine Davies. It was a wonderful day. Most importantly, the event demonstrated to a very excluded and often discriminated against community that senior people locally, and from Whitehall, thought they mattered. Dylan Harrison quickly followed up the opening with an offer of transport for the children on the site to local early years provision. It is unlikely that such an offer, so clearly good for the children, would have been accepted had the earlier work not been done. Harrison had first established trust; he had created an environment that would encourage parents to do the best things for their children.

Getting going: leadership from Whitehall

Tessa Jowell was now chairing the Ministerial Steering Group for Sure Start. She had chaired the CSR that resulted in the creation of Sure Start and, as a public health minister, she was deeply committed to the programme and, in particular, was interested in the very early years. In interview, she expressed her passion for the programme and for its emphasis on very young children: "I want to smell the babies". Like the original group overseeing the CSR, the Steering Group had ministers from several government departments in addition to the Department of Health (DH): the Treasury, DfEE, Department of Social Security (DSS), Department of the Environment, Transport and the Regions (DETR), Home Office and Department for Culture, Media and Sport (DCMS). Most of the ministers on the group were women, and the women were more regular in their attendance at Steering Group meetings than the men. The group met about every two months and had at least four or five ministers attending at most of the meetings. For Tessa Jowell, this was a very small part of a big ministerial job, but the one she felt most passionate about, and on which she spent considerable amounts of time. For all of the ministers, this was their comfort zone, one of the few responsibilities they had that was genuinely enjoyable. The meetings were much less formal than inter-ministerial groups had been in the past, with civil servants and ministers sitting together, and all contributing. Sure Start was an extremely popular programme and there was a natural desire to see things happen, and happen quickly. A programme that was meant to deliver better outcomes for very young children as they reached adolescence and adulthood was expected to have demonstrable effects in weeks and months.

The first reshuffle: a new minister and a new direction

While programme approvals and implementation were moving along, albeit very slowly, the first of many political changes took place. In October 1999, the Prime Minister decided on a small reshuffle. Among the changes, Tessa Jowell was moved from the DH to the DfEE. She was replaced at the DH by Yvette Cooper. This presented a real problem for the newly created cross-departmental Sure Start Unit. Tessa Jowell had been a staunch supporter of the new initiative, genuinely loved it and, by her own background, knew the policy context very well. She wanted to hold on to the programme in her new role. David Blunkett, still Secretary of State for Education and Employment, supported this idea. However, it would have meant, very early on, losing the cross-departmental nature of the unit, as Tessa Jowell was moving to Blunkett's department. This would have been a real loss. Being wholly owned by one department would have seriously changed the nature of the programme. Sure Start was about joined-up government, working across boundaries and collaboration at all levels. Losing the cross-departmental arrangements at the centre of government would set a dangerous precedent down the delivery chain. However, there were some serious tactical and protocol problems in stopping it. It would have been difficult for Rob Smith, my superior at the DfEE, to support my attempts to maintain the cross-government arrangements with the DH. He was a senior official working for David Blunkett. Norman Glass, still the lead official at the Treasury on Sure Start, did not have the same constraints, as he worked neither for David Blunkett, nor for Frank Dobson, the Secretary of State for Health. Glass was very keen to keep the DH on board.

Geoff Mulgan proved to be another important ally at the time. As a great supporter of new cross-cutting arrangements, he also saw the importance of keeping the DH formally involved. After about 10 days, the issue was resolved with a note from Jeremy Heywood, then the Prime Minister's Principal Private Secretary. Yvette Cooper took over as day-to-day minister in charge, reporting to David Blunkett on Sure Start business. However, their relationship was never as warm as that between Blunkett and Jowell. Sure Start's honeymoon was over, although the first few years of partnership between the DfEE and DH were relatively calm. A harbinger for the future was that officials at the DH did not lead the effort to maintain the Sure Start link for Yvette Cooper. It was mainly officials at the Sure Start Unit, the Treasury and support from Number 10 that argued for the continued link with the DH.

The ministerial changes signalled the first of many shifts in Sure Start policy. Yvette Cooper was an economist; her husband, Ed Balls, was a senior political adviser at the Treasury. Both were very committed to reducing child poverty through employment. At the same time, Margaret Hodge was the minister in charge of childcare and early education at the DfEE. Her responsibilities included the National Childcare Strategy and, with that, the Neighbourhood Nursery Initiative. She looked with understandable envy at the generous capital investment in SSLPs that was not always being used to support the childcare strategy. The 2000 CSR was the beginning of what came to be considered the capture of the programme by the employability agenda. The first set of PSA targets for Sure Start had no specific requirements either on improving employment rates in Sure Start areas, or increasing the quantity of childcare for working parents. This was to change.

The 2000 Comprehensive Spending Review: bigger and better?

As explained earlier, the first year of formal operation for Sure Start was 1999/2000. Planning began for the next CSR at virtually the beginning of the second year (2000/01). Most programmes were taking about three years to become fully operational. By April 2000, barely 60 programmes had been approved and were just starting to spend money. The National Evaluation of Sure Start reports that spending for each programme in year one was on average £150,000. By the fourth year, average spend per programme rose to £700,000 (Meadows, 2007, p 21). Given the low level of spend, it was evident by April 2000 that very few services for families were actually operational, even in the programmes that had been approved. We were being asked to make recommendations on the next phase of the programme with virtually no knowledge of whether any of this ambitious new way of delivering early years services would have any impact at all. The evaluation had not yet started. Yet there was enormous pressure from ministers to expand the programme. The confidence at the time that Sure Start was already a success was extraordinary. An election was likely to be held in the spring of 2001 and expanding Sure Start would make a great story.

Officials were almost universally against expansion. Norman Glass in describing the enthusiasm for Sure Start among ministers wrote in *The Guardian*:

> So well was it received that, 18 months later, as the Treasury Official with principal responsibility for Sure Start alongside my DfES colleagues, I was having to argue against its immediate expansion, on the grounds that it would be better to accumulate some experience of running it first. (By October 1999, when I discussed the scheme with the Chancellor, there were only two local projects actually up and running.) (Glass, 2005)

In an effort to stave off, or at least limit, expansion, civil servants presented ministers with three options for Sure Start in the 2000 CSR:

- keep to the current plan of 250 programmes;
- expand by an additional 125 programmes; or
- expand by an additional 250 programmes.

It was hoped that ministers would behave as most people do when offered three options, go for the middle one. Ministers went for the third option, doubling the number of programmes and enormously increasing the funding allocation for Sure Start. Total funding for the first three years was £450 million. Table 4.1 shows the enormous increase in funding from the original 1998 allocation to the announcement just two years later.

Table 4.1: Sure Start budget allocation 1999–2004

Year	1999/2000	2000/01	2001/02	2002/03	2003/04
Budget	£80 million	£184 million	£284 million[a]	£449 million	£499 million

[a] This figure includes £100 million of rolled-forward underspent funds.

In keeping with the CSR principle of increased flexibility on unspent funds, not only was Sure Start allowed to keep the underspend from its first two years, its new baseline for future spending reviews was nearly £500 million, the amount allocated for 2003/04, the final year of the period covered by the 2000 CSR.

The expansion meant Sure Start programmes could potentially reach one half of poor under-fours in England, compared to the one third meant to be reached by the first 250 programmes. It would mean setting up programmes not just in the poorest 20% of wards, but in the poorest 30% of wards. Doubling the number of programmes would not mean doubling the number of poor children reached, in that the new programme areas would have fewer poor children in them, compared to the child population. More children would be reached, but a smaller proportion of them would be poor.

It was clear that to achieve the target of 500 programmes operational by March 2004 we would need faster processes for programme approval, and we would need to assist programmes in getting started much more quickly. Yet again, optimism and politics overruled the more measured and cautious approach recommended by officials. At local level, the programme was also proving to be enormously popular. The only complaint that ministers were hearing from Members of Parliament about Sure Start was 'Why can't my constituency have one?'. The pressure to expand was enormous.

While civil servants were worried about the speed and quality of implementation, let alone whether the programme would work at all, the liberal press welcomed the new investment. Under the banner headline, 'Children in the Poorest Families Get Help to Succeed at School', Denny wrote in *The Guardian*:

> The government's determination to tackle child poverty and social exclusion was underlined yesterday when Gordon Brown announced a cross department initiative to help the poorest and most vulnerable children in Britain.
>
> In an effort to break the cycle of disadvantage, the chancellor has doubled investment in the Sure Start programme which aims to improve the life chances of under-fives by ensuring they are ready to learn when they begin school. (Denny, 2000)

The new CSR was not just about money. It also meant a review of the original PSA targets. When spending plans were announced in 1998, the PSA regime was very new, and targets were actually finalised a few months after the funding announcements. For the 2000 CSR, there was a much better alignment of the announcement of financial allocations and PSA targets. There were to be fewer PSA targets, and a stronger emphasis on outcome rather than output targets.

As was mentioned in Chapter Three, one of the key challenges in meeting the PSA targets was the difficulty in data collection at local level. This problem was compounded by a target about which Sure Start interventions were unlikely to improve outcomes. The target on reducing low birth weight proved to be particularly problematic. Low birth weight is a very powerful indicator of child outcomes, but it is a target almost impossible to shift given the nature of SSLPs. Contact must be made pre-conception or very early in pregnancy. Health agencies were usually reluctant to provide data on newly pregnant women to Sure Start staff. For the 2000 CSR, the low birth weight target was replaced with a specific target on reducing smoking in pregnancy. This target also proved very difficult for the same reasons: lack of data from primary care providers made contact with women early in pregnancy highly unlikely. There could be contact with second and subsequent pregnancies if the mother was using Sure Start services for older children, but if a woman was pregnant for the first time, there was little chance of contact with local Sure Start services until weeks or months after the baby was born. Teen mothers, the group likely to be both first-time mothers and the most disadvantaged, would be least likely to have contact with the programmes while pregnant. The evaluation results described in Chapter Eight will go into this issue in more detail.

Ameliorating the impact of poverty, or reducing the number of poor children?

The main findings of the research review that led to Sure Start were about the inextricable correlation between child poverty, particularly if experienced persistently in the very early years of childhood, and poor outcomes in adult life. The main thrust of Sure Start, and that of most of the large children's charities at the time, was to ameliorate the effects of poverty on young children with compensatory programmes. The Prime Minister's announcement in March 1999 to end child poverty in a generation required an alignment with wider government policy on poverty.

Ministerial priorities were shifting. Yvette Cooper was surprised that there was little link between the New Deal for Lone Parents programme, encouraging employment among single mothers, and Sure Start. Likewise, Margaret Hodge, tasked with increasing available childcare, thought some of the capital investment in Sure Start should be for day care facilities for working parents. Both Carey Oppenheim, then the childcare lead at Number 10, and Ed Miliband, the Sure Start lead at the Treasury, were asking similar questions. I accompanied them on their first visit to a Sure Start programme in Tilbury in Essex. They were surprised that the welfare-to-work agenda, and particularly the Prime Minister's March 1999 announcement on the intention to end child poverty in a generation, was not yet visible in the planned services and capital investment through Sure Start. The political classes were joining up agendas more quickly than either the civil servants or, indeed, the local boards running the programmes.

Hence, a new target was added to an existing objective:

> Objective IV: strengthening families and communities
> Reduce the number of 0–3 year old children in Sure Start areas living in households where no one is working by 2004. (HMT, 2000)

The introduction of the employment target proved to be unpopular with SSLP managers and has remained politically contentious. Both Tessa Jowell and David Blunkett commented on this change in their interviews for this book. Jowell remarked:

> "Nobody got the bull's eye that Sure Start was originally intended to be about nurture. Because the focus moved from babies to 2–5 year olds, it became childcare and education. And then the best way to deal with the poverty of these mums is to get them out to work. Bingo! You have completely recast it from this very very precious early concept of nurture, to an arm of the welfare-to-work strategies."

Blunkett, too, was concerned about the shift to childcare:

> "I saw the old Soviet-style day care centres, you know, everybody sleeping in rows at the same time of day, and I didn't want that, I wanted something very different.... I think Gordon was interested in mass childcare partly as an economic driver."

The controversy on the employability agenda is a continuous theme throughout the Sure Start story. In an oral evidence session of the House of Commons Children, Schools and Families Committee on Sure Start Children's Centres in November 2009, I was asked the following by Karen Buck, MP for Kensington and Chelsea:

> One of the criticisms that has also come through recently ... is the extent to which the employability agenda and the drive for child care expansion to enable parents to work has squeezed out the emphasis on the relationship between parents and their very young children and the child centred approach. Do you think that's true? Is it inevitable? Is it important to keep those two in balance? (House of Commons, 2009, p 33)

My own view at the time was, and continues to be, that it was right to encourage employment, and to ensure that capital investment was suitable for childcare. But, again, there was a tension between the government's desire for local control and its own overarching policy goals. SSLP managers said that parents were not asking for childcare, and usually showed little interest in employment. My response to these comments was twofold. First, even if the current cohort of parents were not wanting childcare, the capital investment would be for several more years to come, and therefore needed to be flexible enough to respond to changing needs. It would be difficult to add suitable space for childcare later, while easy to use such space for other things if the current group of users were not wanting childcare. Second, and probably more important, our role was to raise aspirations, suggest new ideas and provide people with opportunities to change and improve their circumstances. Our role was changing from ameliorating the effects of family poverty on poor children to making families less poor. Exactly as Karen Buck had suggested, however, parent support should not be instead of employment support; both go hand in hand.

There is no doubt that, even with what seemed a very short period of time, and before much was actually happening on the ground, Sure Start was changing. In part, we were learning what a demanding task we were asking of local people. The problems identified in the original Comprehensive Spending Review on Services for Young Children were about a fragmented and patchy service covering an area of social policy that had been pretty much neglected. There was a naive view that all these problems, and the issues identified through the *Modernising Government* agenda as well, would be solved through Sure Start. I often thought to myself that the appropriate metaphor was *Sure Start* and *global warming*. There was no way that this initiative was going to fulfil all the dreams imbued in it by ministers. Sure Start felt like a pilot project, albeit highly innovative in its inception, governance arrangements and model of tight–loose oversight from Whitehall. However, the implications of a pilot are usually that it is small-scale, with tight evaluation and with at least the possibility that it will fail. Such was the optimism at the time that this simply was not considered. Sure Start was paving the way for even bigger and more far-reaching changes to the nature of children's services under the banner of Every Child Matters. But, first, there was the enormously complex task of setting up the evaluation and another, significantly more radical, spending review to come.

FIVE

How will we know it works?

This chapter will describe the way in which the evaluation of Sure Start was set up, and some of the key controversies surrounding the evaluation. Given the size of the evaluation, and the likely attention such an evaluation would get in the research community, it is not surprising that deciding who would do it and, more importantly, how it would be designed proved enormously difficult. There was political conflict, personality conflicts and deeply held scientific arguments about the evaluation of Sure Start. Indeed, Sir Michael Rutter, one of Britain's most esteemed scientists, believed that the way in which the programme was set up made it impossible to evaluate, and that the 'undermining of the evaluation was political and deliberate' (Rutter, 2007, p 203). The key debate was in two parts – the design of the programme itself and the design of the evaluation:

- To what extent should the design of the programme be determined by whether or not it could be scientifically proven to work? There are key features of the original design of Sure Start that made evaluation extremely difficult. It was argued by academics that the design should be determined not by what was already known, but by what could be learned through rigorous evaluation; they argued consistently for a standardised model of inputs that could be tested using the gold standard of evaluation – a randomised control trial (RCT).
- Given that both ministers and civil servants agreed to a programme design that could not easily conform to the standard of rigorous evaluation, how would we know if it worked, and over what period of time? Could the most rigorous form of evaluation – an RCT – be used given the design we had chosen?

The evaluation story presents a classic case study in clashes between a number of cultures: a scientific community that wanted its research to stand up to peer rigour; a political class who could not conceive of Sure Start not being a success; a wide range of stakeholder organisations who wanted to make sure that their version of what would work would be proven to be true; and a divided civil service community, with the professional analysts wanting a rigorous credible evaluation, but the policy officials, under intense pressure from ministers, wanting to get the programmes going with visible change on the ground and the money being used as intended.

Why was Sure Start so difficult to evaluate?

The purpose of evaluation of any programme is to test if resources spent on a particular activity are achieving a particular intended outcome. An even more difficult question is whether the same outcome could be achieved with the deployment of fewer or different resources, or, indeed, what would happen if nothing was done. The fundamentally important principle in programme evaluation is the unambiguous connection between a particular activity, input or intervention and the consequences or outcomes resulting from the activity. The scientific gold standard of evaluation is the RCT. A group of candidates are selected for a standardised intervention. The group is randomly divided into individuals who get the treatment and those who do not. For this design to work, it is critically important that the intervention is the same for all those receiving it and the measurement for change is the same, so that clear measurable objectives in advance of treatment are vital. Those who receive the treatment and those who do not are measured before and after to establish whether the intervention had the intended impact, that is, a positive outcome. The size of the impact is also important. If there was minimal change, then was the cost of the intervention really value for money?

The point of an RCT is comparing individuals or groups who are identical in every respect except that one gets the intervention and one does not. Only if the individuals are the same in all other respects can the difference measured after the intervention be attributed to the intervention. However, social interventions never happen in a vacuum. A wide range of other circumstances may affect change in individuals or populations. The key to an evaluation design that does not use randomised controls is to reduce the number of other factors that may have affected the change. In the case of Sure Start, this was incredibly challenging. Four fundamental aspects of the design of Sure Start made it almost impossible to evaluate and certainly not suitable for an RCT evaluation design:

- First, the insistence on engagement of parents in Sure Start Local Programmes (SSLPs) on what would be delivered meant that Sure Start was not one 'intervention', but several hundred different interventions. It would, therefore, be impossible to define a standardised treatment.

• Second, we were not allocating the intervention randomly, either on an individual family basis or an area basis; the programme was being rolled out and all families in the areas had access to it. Given the emphasis on community engagement in the design of SSLPs, it would have been difficult to then randomly exclude some of those who had participated in the planning from actually using the services.

• Third, there was a measurement problem. Sure Start was intended to address the fragmentation of early years services through service integration. It was implicitly assumed that integration would lead to better outcomes, but service integration is very hard to measure and even more difficult to link to particular outcomes (Waldfogel, 1997, pp 463–84). Furthermore, the Treasury-led Review on services for young children (HMT, 1998b) found that services were very patchy, so the particular pattern of service delivery pre-existing Sure Start in each of the local areas was widely variable, meaning that there would be no clear baseline from which to measure more or less integration.

• Lastly, measurement of outcomes was a problem, as was the case in measuring progress on Sure Start's Public Service Agreement (PSA) targets. Data at SSLP level were patchy and of mixed quality. This was compounded by the idiosyncratic way that each local SSLP area was defined. Measurement of change before and after Sure Start for individual families, or, indeed, comparison to similar families in other non-Sure Start areas, would be difficult.

These four factors alone would have been challenging. In addition to these issues, the programme doubled in size barely 18 months after it was set up, increasing the difficulty of finding comparably poor areas with which to compare SSLP areas. Also, changes of ministers meant that the priorities and, indeed, the tone of communication from Whitehall were frequently changing. The last two issues were not anticipated in setting up the evaluation, but certainly made its management very difficult.

The intention of Sure Start was to improve outcomes by improving service quality and coordination for all young children in a particular area, not just those engaged with Sure Start. The variety of services, both existing and newly created through Sure Start funding, made the linking of any particular service to any particular family extremely difficult. Within a Sure Start area, a small number of families could be using a very large number of services; but another group of families may be using hardly any. Those not using services may not need them, or may need them but not want them. So there were another set of questions: who uses which services and how often? The type of interventions that benefit from RCTs have standardised inputs and standardised dosage models, that is, how much of the input they get. Indeed, many of the RCT-tested parenting programmes turn out to be enormously successful, but only for those who participate in them and stay for the prescribed number of weeks for a set number of sessions. This is commonly referred to as *treatment on the treated* model. Sure Start had no notion of a *prescribed dosage* for a particular problem leading to improvement. The model of evaluation would have to be an *intention to treat* model, a random selection of all those for whom the treatment is made available, compared to a selection of a similar group who did not have access. Given that ministers had already rejected the idea of any children and families in SSLP areas being prevented from access to services, the only solution was to find equally poor children living in non-Sure Start areas and compare them to the Sure Start children. Furthermore, we wanted better child cognitive development, better parenting, more social cohesion and better health, and we wanted all these improved outcomes from a complex package of inputs designed to suit local communities and, indeed, individual families. It would have been very difficult to find two children under four receiving exactly the same Sure Start *treatment* even within the same SSLP, let alone across 250 programmes.

An added difficulty was that Sure Start was operating as an area-based initiative. Sure Start was only one of a large number of area-based initiatives set up in the early years of the Labour government. Because almost all of the area-based initiatives were aimed at poor areas, there was significant overlap. There were simply not enough poor areas to go around. So disentangling the impact of Sure Start from that of the Education Action Zone, the Health Action Zone or the New Deal for Communities would also be difficult.

The US interventions that were looked at as models for Sure Start had all been designed as small-scale, experimental pilot programmes, with very clear aims, standardised delivery mechanisms and evaluations through RCTs over a number of years. Indeed, some had been operating for well over 20 years with a standardised delivery model. Not only were ministers unwilling to specify a standardised model, they were also unwilling to wait 10 or 20 years for results. It was already well established from US programmes that early intervention with very young children living in poverty had a positive long-term impact. The key message taken from the US programmes was about early intervention and about working with parents and children. However, as argued earlier in Chapter Three, Sure Start was replicating little else of the basic features of what had worked in the US. Hence, it would not be sensible to replicate the evaluation methodology of an RCT for such a diverse programme. Furthermore, an RCT was considered almost unethical; so convinced were ministers of the future success of Sure Start that they were unwilling to deny some children access to what they were sure was going to be extremely beneficial.

Sure Start started out quite large and grew in size before the evaluation was formally contracted. It was intended to be different in different areas, and not only grew in size, but changed in emphasis and culture, over its first few years. The academic experts advising the Treasury on the design for Sure Start consistently argued against the proposed design partly because of the challenges of evaluation, but also because they believed adherence to a proven model would have better chance of success. The policymakers and voluntary-sector stakeholders, however, were not to be shifted from their emphasis on community and local diversity. There was an unshakeable belief that Sure Start could not fail. A solution would have to found to the evaluation problems. The challenges set by the design and, indeed, the often-voiced argument that Sure Start could not be evaluated did not deter many very high-quality academics from competing to win the contract to evaluate Sure Start. Not only was this a very high-profile contract, but it was comparatively generous. While no specific amount was specified in the tender document, the scope and scale described in the invitation to tender was consistent with the indicative budget provision we had made, around £12 million.

Establishing the process

For all of the reasons just cited, it was decided to commission a feasibility study first before commissioning the Sure Start evaluation. The Sure Start Evaluation Development Project, carried out between July and November 1999, would give recommendations to solve the thorny problem of testing the efficacy of Sure Start. A broad team of academics led by John Bynner at the Centre for Longitudinal Studies' Institute of Education won the tender to carry out the study with the assurances that this would not disbar them from competing for the full evaluation. They came up with a set of questions that would need to be answered using several overlapping forms of evaluation:

- What was the nature of the population (children and families) recruited into the local Sure Start Projects?
- How was Sure Start implemented at the local level and how are its goals and strategies evolving?
- What was the immediate impact of Sure Start locally and nationally?
- What were the longer term effects of Sure Start?
- What were the particular factors about Sure Start projects that made a difference, project features, nature of implementation, type of area?
- What were the relative costs and benefits of the Sure Start programme nationally? (Bynner et al, 1999, p 22)

As policymakers, we wanted to know what aspects of Sure Start, and under what specific conditions, would work to improve outcomes for which children. The Development Project also came up with some important operational principles for the evaluation that were in keeping with the ethos of the programme:

> In developing the design, a number of principles have been established, the most important of which is that in the collection of data from parents and children, involving the local teams, sensitivity to the local context, and the need to minimize the burden of informants are at a premium. The success of the evaluation will also be critically dependent on the co-ordination of local evaluation and national evaluation work within a single collaborative framework. To guarantee credibility of the findings of the evaluation, it should also be seen as operating separately from the Sure Start Unit. Rights to ownership of the data collected, and to publish independently of the Unit are also important to the evaluation's success. (Bynner et al, 1999, p v)

The Development Project Team wanted to ensure two things: that the evaluation itself did not prove too burdensome or intrusive on SSLPs; and that there would be complete independence from government on the research. It would be extremely important not just for academic credibility, but also for confidence in results by the press and specialist commentators, that the evaluation was rigorous and free from interference by those who would be most embarrassed by poor results.

Who won, and why?

The scientific arguments about the evaluation were difficult. The political and personal conflicts were even more stressful. Personal friendships, high-profile academics and the role of ministers in procurement of contracts all came into play.

Given the complexities of the issues, the Sure Start Unit was clear, and the Development Project supported the view, that it was highly unlikely that any one institution would have the range of expertise needed to evaluate Sure Start. We were looking for a consortium, not a single organisation. We were expecting most of the prominent social science research departments and organisations in the UK to be represented at the early stages of selection, and, in the event, over 20 consortia made bids to undertake the evaluation. Four of these came through in the final selection process. However, there were added complications for two of the four front-runners. By the time the invitation to tender for the full evaluation went out, Norman Glass had left the civil service to become Chief Executive of the National Centre for Social Research (NatCen). NatCen, a highly regarded research organisation in Britain, was very keen to be involved in the evaluation. NatCen had been part of the team that had done the Development Project, so, according to prior agreement, could not be excluded. But questions were raised about the appropriateness of Glass being involved in the evaluation of Sure Start given the role he had played in establishing the programme while he was a senior civil servant at the Treasury. Glass took steps to ensure that he had no involvement in the tender process and distanced himself until after the tender had been awarded.

A consortium that included Birkbeck College also emerged as a front-runner. Sir Tim O'Shea, then Master at Birkbeck, had recruited Jay Belsky, who had written extensively in the US on the risks of early group care on babies and young children. At the time, he was a controversial figure, particularly in the US, but not yet well known to civil servants in Britain. While there was controversy about Glass's involvement, there was also concern about Belsky's involvement given his position on day care, which did not sit well at the time with the government's National Childcare Strategy. Consequently, key figures in each of the front-running teams for the evaluation were creating noise in a system that was meant to be completely open, fair and free from political involvement. In keeping with traditional government procurement rules, the process used was to agree with ministers a basic budget for the evaluation, the specifications in the invitation to tender and the criteria which would be used to select the final choice, but otherwise keep ministers clear of the decision.

At the same time, the Economic and Social Research Council had awarded a major grant to John Bynner's Centre for Longitudinal Studies to run the Millennium Cohort Study (MCS), a longitudinal study of children born in the year 2000. The DfEE was also partly funding the MCS. Given the arguments about the evaluation design, it was thought that the MCS would be a good source of comparison children for the Sure Start evaluation. Hence, part of the Sure Start evaluation requirement was to demonstrate how the group chosen would work collaboratively with the MCS. The arrangement was that a front-runner would be chosen and then, depending on that group's ability to provide a satisfactory plan to work collaboratively with the MCS, the contract would be awarded.

It was extremely important not only to select the best consortium, but to be seen to be fair and to ensure that the work done by the selected group would be robust enough to stand up to very tough academic as well as public scrutiny. All the bids were subjected to rigorous independent peer review. To strengthen the expertise available, I wrote to Sir Michael Rutter to ask if he would be willing to be a part of the panel selecting the best evaluation team. Sir Michael was one of the most vocal objectors to the basic design of Sure Start, saying it could not be evaluated with any certainty or rigour. He also had ethical objections to Norman Glass having any role in the evaluation given his involvement in its origins. Rutter refused to take part in the panel selection, but agreed to be a member of the expert oversight group that would advise the winning team.

In the event, both front-running teams were invited to come back with revised proposals. The Treasury, who had been insistent on a rigorous evaluation as part of the conditions of funding Sure Start, also asked for presentations from the two front-running teams, and made their views on their preferred group known to the selection panel. Independent academic peer reviewers also advised the panel.

The Birkbeck consortium was selected by civil servants as the preferred group. They then needed to put together a proposal with the MCS group to ensure that they could work together effectively. John Bynner, in charge of the MCS, had also been involved in the NatCen bid, so agreeing a way of working together was not straightforward and was likely to take some weeks. Meanwhile, the other unsuccessful bidders had to be informed. Yet another personal issue arose. Professor June Thoburn from the University of East Anglia was a major player in one of the unsuccessful bids. She was very close friends with Baroness

Patricia Hollis who was on the Sure Start Ministerial Steering Group. We did not want one of our ministers to hear from a friend, possibly on Saturday morning in the gym, about the outcome of this very high-profile contest. So we decided to write a note of information to all the ministers on the Ministerial Steering Group informing them that the Birkbeck team was the front-runner.

The Birkbeck team was ecstatic. Nobody else was. Glass was convinced not only that we had made a dreadful error, but that interference from Sir Michael Rutter had played a major role. It had not, but Glass immediately sent emails to former Treasury colleagues berating them about the decision. Margaret Hodge, Early Years Minister and also on the Ministerial Steering Group, also thought we had made a dreadful mistake, largely because of Belsky's views on early childcare, but also because she thought the team was not balanced, being over-represented on social work expertise and thin on education.

The Birkbeck offer was not yet formalised, but they had been informed because they had to get started on the collaboration arrangements with the MCS. It would still have been possible to rescind the decision. But the second choice team included NatCen. Given Glass's very vocal dissatisfaction, we could not just go for number two. We would have had to redo the whole process, taking at least another six months, and it was highly unlikely we would have gotten any new bids. Most of the eminent academics had already had a go. The instruction from ministers to hold up the process while further considerations were made meant some of us had a pretty miserable Christmas. A huge amount of work had already gone into the process of choosing an evaluation team, and the idea of facing a repeat for several months in the future while trying desperately to get the programme going was an awful thought indeed. A further irony was that I had been friends with Tim O'Shea for many years, and we were clearly on opposite sides of a very high fence trimmed with broken glass. O'Shea was, understandably, promising a huge amount of bad publicity if the deal fell through.

Was it the right decision?

In the end, ministers agreed to the Birkbeck consortium in January 2001. Some changes were negotiated that helped, including putting Professor Edward Melhuish in overall charge and adding an education expert to the team. Ministers continued to have their doubts about the evaluation. In my view, they never really came to grips with the complexity of evaluating Sure Start and so were continually uncomfortable with the mixed messages from the evaluation. They were particularly uncomfortable with what it could not tell us. No research design can answer all questions, and good designs always generate more interesting questions. Chapter Eight will provide a detailed description of the evaluation results and the impact they had on Sure Start.

The main criteria for the choice was that Birkbeck presented a research design that would periodically give knowledge about what was and was not working, on the basis of which we could change the programme as we went along. This, indeed, did happen, although not all changes to the programme were based on evidence from the evaluation.

Michael Rutter played a very valuable role on the expert peer review group, as did a number of academics who generously gave their expertise even though they were from teams that tendered but were not successful. Rutter's view on the team selected, after working with them over a number of years, was positive:

> given the constraints imposed by government, this was as rigorous and careful an evaluation as could be undertaken. The research team are to be congratulated on their high-quality research. As a consequence, there is every reason to trust the research findings. (Rutter, 2007, pp 197–209)

There is no way of knowing if the right decision was made as we have no way of knowing what any of the others seeking the contract would have achieved. I would tend to agree with Michael Rutter that, given the complexity of the task, Melhuish and Belsky and the rest of the National Evaluation of Sure Start Team did an excellent job. I disagree with Rutter that the government did not want a serious and thoughtful evaluation. Ministers and officials were intensely interested in the emerging evidence from the evaluation, and, as will be shown in future chapters, lessons from the evaluation were continually used to improve Sure Start.

As to the question of the fundamental programme design flaws, this is still a subject of argument in academic and service delivery circles. In my view, some of those who championed particular evidenced-based interventions were arguing for a particular product they themselves were offering. They wanted their model everywhere, and argued that Sure Start had wasted public money by not insisting from the beginning on a fixed manualised model that could be evaluated by an RCT. My view is that we could have been somewhat more prescriptive, but also that we were not introducing an *intervention*, we were trying to achieve *systems reform*. An intervention is usually delivered to solve a particular problem for a particular group. Sure Start was responding to a multiple set of issues affecting a large and disparate group living in areas with highly variable services. We started with an argument about patchy, uncoordinated services of mixed quality. We wanted to improve quality, improve coordination and fill in gaps so that any family with a child under four in a Sure Start area would experience a seamless, high-quality and integrated service. Reforming the system does not mean doing the same everywhere, it means working with the current system to try to even out the inequities to ensure, as far as possible, that gaps in provision are filled and the gaps in outcomes are narrowed. It was and, indeed, continues to be a huge assumption that this would improve outcomes. In retrospect, it was incredibly brave and innovative to try to establish a positive relationship between such a radical system reform and particular child outcomes. This really had not been done before, and would prove really difficult. Indeed, while the impact part of the evaluation study turned out to be robust, the implementation study that may have illuminated more about the nature of service integration was weak. Hence, we learned a lot about outcomes for children, but we are still struggling with what the particularly well-performing SSLPs did differently from the others to achieve better results.

In Chapter Eight, the evaluation results will be described, as well as the huge impact initial results would have on Sure Start. The next chapter describes some of the huge and radical changes to children's services and to Sure Start that took place between 2002 and 2004.

SIX

Stroppy adolescence

The next part of the Sure Start story is set against a complex set of interconnecting changes at the heart of government. All of these changes affected Sure Start in some way, and all had a much wider impact on children's and broader social policy. A series of significant events and publications were critical to the transformation of Sure Start over the subsequent five years, as well as to the delivery of children's services across England:

- A Labour victory in the general election of 2001 was followed by a reorganisation of the DfEE and a change of Secretary of State. A new government department, the Department for Work and Pensions (DWP), was set up with the transfer of employment responsibilities from the DfEE, now called the Department for Education and Skills (DfES), with Estelle Morris as Secretary of State.

- *Tackling Child Poverty* (HMT, 2001, pp vi–vii) was published as part of the Pre-Budget Report in the autumn of 2001. This Treasury document argued that both fiscal and social policies together would be needed to achieve the aim of ending child poverty.

- A major interdepartmental review of childcare was carried out. It recommended the merger of childcare, early years and Sure Start, and also recommended a bigger role for local authorities in the design and delivery of all early years and care policy, including childcare for school-aged children. The 2002 Comprehensive Spending Review (CSR) followed this advice, changing the joint departmental responsibilities for Sure Start from the DfES and Department of Health (DH), to the DfES and DWP, merging the Sure Start Unit with the Early Years and Childcare Units.

- Major changes in the machinery of government took place in the summer of 2003 with the setting up of a new department for children and families, which brought together for the first time education, children's social care and family policy, with aspects of family law. However, the restructured department would still be called the DfES for some years to come.

- A new minister of state post was created, the Minister for Children, which would be the first minister of state-level post in government with no responsibilities other than children's policy, with Margaret Hodge as the first post-holder.

- Finally, a radical new approach to all children's services was developed – the Every Child Matters agenda.

Labour wins again

The Labour Party manifesto for the 2001 election mentions Sure Start once. This is not surprising. Compared to overall government activity and spend, even on education and care, Sure Start was still small beer. Moreover, the nature of Sure Start would have made it very difficult to slot in under any particular heading: health, education, regeneration or tax and benefits. One of the problems of *joined-up* policies is that they do not reflect the basic organisation of government at national or local level. But the 2001 manifesto, *Ambitions for Britain*, is strongly positioned on children, both in service terms and in wider tax, benefit and welfare-to-work terms. Two areas stand out in particular: the next stage of education reform in secondary schools, with promises of more funding and more teachers; and several policy commitments supporting Blair's March 1999 pledge to end child poverty in a generation. The manifesto promised something for all children – improved secondary schools – and something particularly ambitious for poor children – ending poverty.

For the under-fives, there are two pledges:

- By 2004 every three-year-old will be entitled to a free nursery place in the private, voluntary or statutory sector. OfSTED will help drive up standards. Children with special educational needs will have those needs identified earlier. We will continue to provide services which integrate early years education with childcare.
- By 2004 we will have 100 Early Excellence Centres as beacons of good practice providing care and education for children from 0–5; we will set up 500 Sure Start Centres in disadvantaged areas to support children's early development; and we will provide an extra 100,000 places offering wraparound care linked to early education. (Labour Party, 2001, p 18)

It is important to note that the main pledge – extending free nursery education to three-year-olds – is somewhat different from the 1997 pledge of free nursery education for four-year-olds in that the government explicitly encouraged diversity of provision across the public, voluntary and private sectors. This is an important philosophical change in that it signals a move to a wider choice for parents to use their free nursery *education* offer as part of the hours of childcare needed to enable parents to work. It also signals a desire to develop a co-funded market in childcare, that is, a system that is paid for by a combination of parental contributions, tax credits and state funding. There is a commitment to 100 Early Excellence Centres and a mention of 500 Sure Start *Centres*, which refers to the planned expansion of the programme announced in the 2000 CSR. It is notable that, even as early as 2001, the term 'Centre' is seen as preferable to 'Local Programmes', probably because it makes more sense to people. From the beginning of Sure Start, it had always been a struggle to precisely describe a 'Sure Start Local Programme', not least because of the diversity of programmes around the country. A building is conceptually easier to imagine. Moreover, most programmes did include a major building, so the terminology of 'Sure Start Centres' became increasingly used. Aside from the reference to placing such centres in disadvantaged areas, there is no explanation of what Sure Start does, or is aiming to do.

The anti-poverty pledges in the manifesto include real cash transfers, as well as policies to help mothers and fathers combine work and family life. The Labour position on work is clear: 'Employment is not just the foundation of affordable welfare. It is the best anti-poverty, anti-crime and pro-family policy yet invented' (Labour Party, 2001, p 24).

This is in sharp contrast to the Conservative manifesto for the same election, which was still somewhat ambivalent about working mothers. Their family policies were limited to: less tax for families, support for marriage and power for parents to choose the best schools for their children. In commenting on childcare, the Tories ascribed the following to the British electorate:

> Families feel more than ever that they are struggling to bring up their children in an environment that is hostile.
>
> They feel it is getting harder to make ends meet, especially when their children are very young. They feel the Government only values childcare if someone else is paid to provide it. (Conservative Party, 2001, p 7)

The Labour position on families and work was to break down every barrier and challenge every excuse not to work. This demanded concerted policy designed to ensure that no one was prevented from working because of unavailable or unaffordable childcare. The Labour commitments in 2001 to encourage employment were numerous: improvements in maternity and paternity leaves, expansion of the children's tax credit, increasing the minimum wage, and expansion of childcare for both under-fives and school-age children:

> Parents need good-quality and affordable childcare if they are to have real choice about work. For the first time, Britain has a National Childcare Strategy covering cost, provision and quality. We have already created 300,000 extra childcare places. By 2004 our target is to have childcare places for 1.6 million children. Our vision is ambitious: safe and reliable childcare nationwide, allowing all parents to combine home and work, confident in the childcare they have chosen. (Labour Party, 2001, p 26)

The relevance of this for Sure Start is twofold. First, childcare was still seen as a means to a particular end – enabling parents to work – and not a *social good* in its own right, that is, the social good of early education. In the manifesto, the two are still seen separately and dealt with in different parts of the document. Second, the wider Sure Start goals of early intervention and service integration are virtually absent from the document. Disadvantage is seen for children almost exclusively through the lens of economics, not the wider range of issues that make social mobility so difficult: social capital, class, the home environment and so on. As will be explained later in this chapter, this narrow view of economic disadvantage was to be broadened within a matter of months in a publication on child poverty accompanying the Pre-Budget Report of autumn 2001. While the manifesto does devote some space to social exclusion, it is largely about the symptoms of exclusion: teen pregnancy, truancy, homelessness and so on. These are the issues that indicate social exclusion was already a big problem. They are also the issues that the US research on high-quality early years provision seemed to indicate were preventable in the future, or at least greatly reduced, if good early years services were in place. They are precisely the social problems that everyone thought Sure Start would ameliorate within 10 or 20 years.

A new department, new ministers and a change of focus

Following the 2001 election, and the start of Labour's second term in office, there was the predictable reshuffle of ministers, but also a significant change in departmental responsibilities. The DfEE became the Department for Education and Skills (DfES) and the employment policy responsibilities of the DfEE were transferred to the new Department for Work and Pensions (DWP). The DWP was essentially the old Department of Social Security, but now with employment and the integrated Jobcentre Plus service added in. The intention was to bring the benefit system, particularly out-of-work benefits, together with the department meant to help people find employment. The new Secretary of State at the DfES was Estelle Morris, previously the Schools Minister at the DfEE. The first Secretary of State at the DWP was Alistair Darling, who was replaced by Andrew Smith in May 2002. Alan Milburn, who had replaced Frank Dobson at the DH in 1999, remained Secretary of State for Health. Yvette Cooper stayed on as Public Health Minister at the DH and so maintained her involvement with Sure Start, but was now reporting to Estelle Morris for Sure Start policy instead of David Blunkett, who was now Home Secretary. Margaret Hodge was promoted to Minister of State for Lifelong Learning and Higher Education. The new minister at the DfES for early years and childcare was Baroness Catherine Ashton. Like her predecessor Margaret Hodge, in the first instance Ashton did not hold the Sure Start brief. This was soon to change.

David Blunkett was the driving force behind the great emphasis on community development for Sure Start. Tessa Jowell was the driving force behind the Sure Start emphasis on babies. Margaret Hodge, while no less committed to Sure Start, was rooted in early learning policy and saw the programme through education eyes. Norman Glass, who had left the Treasury in 2000 to become Chief Executive of the National Centre for Social Research, was the fiercest defender of the Blunkett–Jowell Sure Start vision of local community development action to support mothers and babies. As already mentioned in Chapter Four, Yvette Cooper wanted Sure Start more aligned with welfare-to-work policies, and particularly childcare for working parents. Given the emphasis on child poverty and employment as the only route out of poverty in the 2001 manifesto, it is not surprising that the Policy Unit at Number 10 was getting increasingly concerned about progress on childcare. The ministerial changes, in combination with the huge task of halving child poverty in 10 years, meant that Sure Start needed to take the employment agenda much more seriously. We needed to ensure that every programme was delivering at least some new childcare places, and encouraging every programme to develop relationships at local level with Jobcentre Plus, the arm of the DWP delivering local employment services.

So serious was the concern about the relationship between childcare and employment that, in the reorganisation following the creation of the DWP, there was an argument about where childcare policy should sit: in the new work and pensions department or in the education and skills department. Historically, the childcare unit had been managed within the *employment* side of the DfEE, while early education was managed within the Schools Directorate. Officials at the DWP argued that childcare was so essential to the welfare-to-work agenda for lone parents that it should be transferred with other employment policy responsibilities to the new DWP. At the DfES we argued that what happened to children while they were in childcare was absolutely critical and should not be cut off from other child content-related policy at the DfES. At the time, I commented that people need buses to get to work, so does that mean that the DWP should also carry transport responsibility? We won the argument and kept childcare within the DfES. This debate again underscored the tension in policy intent: childcare enabling parents to work and therefore reduce the numbers of young children growing up in poverty, or early years learning as a route to improve the cognitive and social development of young children to ensure that they achieve in school and therefore have a better chance of employment in adulthood, a much longer-term goal. In other words, were we reducing child poverty or ameliorating its effects. The key to the debate was about funding for quantity (childcare places) or quality (early education). The problem was that quality would cost more. Research was emerging that clearly indicated that quality did matter for child outcomes, and that quality was strongly associated with better-qualified staff. Better-qualified staff tended to be found in the maintained education sector, while childcare staff had fewer qualifications and tended to work in the voluntary or private sectors (Sylva, 2010a, p 82).

Estelle Morris commented with eloquence on the tension between the aims of education for children and employment for parents. She also describes a resolution to the tension. In responding to questions on the relations that the DfES had with the DWP she said:

> "I was always wary of it [the DWP agenda]. I knew their agenda wasn't mine, absolutely. Their agenda was women back to work, it was childcare to get women back to work.

I knew they were not on our side. The things they had to achieve in their department were slightly different in the short term from the things we had to achieve. So it is not a criticism. I could quite see that their objective was to get people back to work, that they needed people to look after the children. The thing was, there's actually not a difference between the two objectives because you can argue it's quite good for children if their parents do go back to work, there's a lot of evidence for that, and they're not going to go back to work without someone to look after the children."

The need for a broader vision on the means to tackle child poverty was recognised within months. The first Pre-Budget Report in the autumn following the election again strongly featured child poverty. This broader vision was not only about economic poverty, but also about the social circumstances that lead to intergenerational poverty. One of the Pre-Budget Report documents published in December 2001 made it clear that tackling child poverty was about the current generation of children living in poverty, and the expectation that their children would not suffer the same fate. This document, co-produced by the Treasury and the relatively new Children and Young People's Unit (CYPU), is more balanced in its approach to employment and wider family services. Four key elements of government policy on children over the next five years are highlighted in the foreword of *Tackling Child Poverty: Giving Every Child the Best Possible Start in Life*, written by Gordon Brown:

- Providing more support for family finances
- Giving priority to children's services, especially health and education
- Offering support to parenting for life
- Pursuing a partnership with the voluntary and community sectors. (HMT, 2001, p iii)

Clearly, employment is part of family finances, as was improving tax credits to make the movement in and out of employment easier. But the inclusion of the other three elements begins to look more like a Sure Start approach: family support, better services and working with the voluntary sector and community. Ironically, as this broader thinking was happening at the Treasury, Sure Start thinking was moving from an emphasis on local community control often through the voluntary and community sectors to a more powerful role for local government.

The Interdepartmental Childcare Review

An interdepartmental review of childcare was commissioned by Number 10 in October 2001. As the Prime Minister himself acknowledges in the foreword to the review, the achievement of universal nursery education for all four year olds, the National Childcare Strategy and Sure Start were already having a real impact on children and families (HMG, 2002). However, services for young children were still operating in silos. Even Sure Start, which was effectively bringing services together at neighbourhood level, was not influencing a more integrated approach outside of its specific programme catchment areas, which usually included around 600 to 900 children under four. Large public investment was going into early education, childcare and Sure Start. But it was believed that the investment could reap more benefit if the synergies across all three areas were exploited. Therefore, the objectives of the review were:

> To assess the future demand and need for childcare, given the trends in labour force participation, and how this compares with current and projected trends in supply;
>
> To assess the effectiveness of different types and qualities of childcare in terms of impacts on child development, educational attainment and labour market outcomes in later life; and
>
> To develop a 10-year vision and strategy for childcare in light of these assessments, including recommendations for improving the effectiveness of delivery mechanisms and bringing greater coherence to existing initiatives (this involved examining different delivery models, funding mechanisms and regulatory approaches). (HMG, 2002, p 63)

The review would require examination of different delivery models, funding mechanisms and regulatory approaches. The key was the need for greater coherence. If the prime rationale for Sure Start was the disadvantage in lifetime opportunities incurred by growing up in poverty, the answer had to be to ameliorate the effects of poverty with compensatory programmes, while, at the same time, reducing poverty by enabling poor families to increase their income through employment and a myriad of tax and benefit changes.

The Childcare Review was published in November 2002, but most of its recommendations were taken up in the 2002 CSR announced the previous summer. While the review was carried out by the Strategy

Unit, which was based in the Cabinet Office, the departments involved in the review were: the DfES, DWP, Treasury and Women and Equality Unit. The review was steered by an inter-ministerial group chaired by Catherine Ashton, then minister in charge of early years and childcare at the DfES. Notably, the DH was not involved.

The findings of the review reflected the findings of the cross-cutting Review on Services for Young Children four years earlier, but looked more broadly to encompass the lone-parent employment and child poverty targets. Unlike the earlier review, it also looked at the need for childcare for school-aged children. As will be discussed in Chapter Seven, this inclusion of childcare for school-aged children proved particularly challenging; bringing the culture of paid-for services into schools was very hard work indeed. Most importantly, the review addressed the importance of childcare investment as a double pay-off, furthering both child development objectives as well as welfare-to-work goals. Three conclusions came out of the review:

- There are very significant payoffs from good quality early intervention for disadvantaged children;
- New investment in childcare is needed to support the Government's employment and poverty targets;
- Investment needs to be backed up by reform. (HMG, 2002, pp 5–6)

There were two recommendations from the review that started the transformation of Sure Start from an innovative, community-based pilot to a mainstream service that would be part of the fabric of local delivery:

- Responsibility for childcare, early years education and Sure Start will be integrated within a new inter-departmental unit, with a total budget of 1.5 billion pounds by 2005/06, to ensure that government policy for children, particularly young children is joined up.
- Greater funding and responsibility for delivery of childcare services will be devolved to local authorities, who are best placed to assess local needs. (HMG, 2002, pp 6–7)

The joining up at the centre made sense to virtually everyone, but the devolution of control for delivery to local authorities proved particularly contentious, both to Sure Start programme managers and to champions of neighbourhood control. Again two issues were challenging the original basis of Sure Start: first, the emphasis on local parental engagement and real power for users of Sure Start to determine what services should be offered seemed to be weakening; and, second, while significantly greater funding was being offered, it looked like the control over that funding would be devolved to local authorities who would have increased flexibility in distribution.

The review recommended the creation of *Children's Centres* for pre-school children in the poorest 20% of areas. As already foreshadowed in the 2001 manifesto (Labour Party, 2001), 'Sure Start Local Programmes' were transforming into 'Sure Start Centres'. The Centres would provide good quality childcare as well as health advice, family support, parental outreach and childminder support. The two key differences between the Children's Centres and the original SSLP model were the departure from the notion of a fixed catchment allowing only families living within a small geographical area to use the services, and the absolute requirement of increasing childcare provision for working parents. These two are related in that the funding models required at least some parents using childcare to be paying for it, albeit with support through tax credits. It was acknowledged that if we stuck very rigidly to the Sure Start catchment areas, the childcare would not be sustainable, even with subsidies. There simply would not be enough paying customers for childcare in these very poor areas. Furthermore, a sensible argument was made using the evidence from the Effective Pre-school and Primary Education project that there were clear developmental gains for poor children of being in high-quality group care with better-off children. The study found that 'Disadvantaged children benefit significantly from good quality pre-school experiences, especially where they attend centres with a mixture of children from different social backgrounds' (Sammons, 2010, p 94).

However, there were downside arguments. The Children's Centre requirements would help ensure that funding was still largely concentrated in poor areas, but the removal of the clear catchment area restrictions, as well as the further expansion of childcare, meant funding would be spread more thinly. It also meant that we were gradually moving from a clear ring-fenced pot of money to be used only in SSLPs to a somewhat larger pot of money that would be dedicated for all early years and childcare support at local government level. Arguments about the *ring-fenced pot* for Sure Start continued and, indeed, became increasingly fierce over the subsequent few years.

The 2002 Comprehensive Spending Review: more big changes

The 2002 CSR began the process of moving Sure Start from a targeted anti-poverty initiative to an integral part of a universal system of care and support for families with young children. The most important of the announcements was the creation of the new Sure Start, Early Years and Childcare Unit at the DfES and the more flexible funding arrangements at local authority level described earlier. Also announced in July as part of the 2002 CSR was the change in cross-departmental responsibility from the DfES and DH to the DfES and DWP. The DWP were delighted with their new prize. Having argued in 2001 about the need to have significant input on childcare policy, they now had clear governance arrangements that made the Sure Start, Early Years and Childcare Unit a joint responsibility.

Barely a month before, in May 2002, Hazel Blears had replaced Yvette Cooper as Minister for Public Health and taken over responsibility for Sure Start, chairing the continuing Ministerial Steering Group that had been set up under Tessa Jowell back in 1999. Blears had worked very hard for a particular Sure Start programme in her constituency, and was clearly committed to the policy area. It is unclear whether the changes in cross-departmental responsibility were agreed with her or, as was often the case in CSR announcements, decided at the Treasury and Number 10 with little consultation with the affected departments. Certainly, senior officials at the DH seemed to be taken by surprise when the changes were announced, but did not argue against them. The absence of representation of the DH on the Childcare Review must have made it much easier to conclude that a DfES–DWP partnership would be more fruitful than a DfES–DH one. Carey Oppenheim was an advisor on childcare in Number 10 at the time. In talking with her about the changes in Sure Start departmental arrangements for this book, she commented as follows:

> "I think it was just very difficult to make cross-cutting issues work very effectively in terms of the machinery of government changes, and often they were sort of put together quite last minute. The idea obviously of going across those two departments was that you would combine issues around employment and income with issues around education and early years services. Why health was left out? Maybe we just felt it was too complicated, it was just another player."

Oppenheim also made an interesting observation about the workings of Number 10. Each of the advisors had links to particular departments. She goes on to say: "The fact that each of us predominantly related to individual departments perhaps made it more difficult to take the best decisions or give the best advice in relation to issues that cut across."

As part of these same changes, the rather informal Sure Start Ministerial Steering Group became a formal cabinet sub-committee chaired by Catherine Ashton with responsibility for the full range of early years and childcare services, not just SSLPs. This made sense given the creation of the integrated unit, but again underlined the blurring of what Sure Start was or would be. Furthermore, a cabinet sub-committee is significantly more formal than a steering group. The agendas and minutes of such committees are under the control of officials at the Cabinet Office and the role of departmental officials is tightly prescribed. While a dedicated committee demonstrated a high-level commitment to early years policy, it also meant some of the informality and energy of the steering group would be lost. Moreover, although Hazel Blears sat on the cabinet sub-committee, DH engagement became even more difficult once the department no longer shared formal governance for Sure Start. We were in grave danger of losing Jowell's babies.

Along with changes in departmental responsibility came different accountability arrangements. Up to this point, the head of the unit sat in the DfES and reported to a minister in the DH; I had been reporting first to Tessa Jowell, then to Yvette Cooper in the DH and, for a very short time, Hazel Blears, while being based in the DfES. We now had a minister who would be based in two departments, and report to two secretaries of state: Andrew Smith at the DWP and Estelle Morris at the DfES. I became the Director of the new Early Years, Childcare and Sure Start Unit, reporting solely to Catherine Ashton. Catherine Ashton was a junior minister in both the DWP and DfES. In the interview for this book, Ashton is clear that the main aim of Sure Start was about early intervention and social mobility. She also acknowledges that the various ministers involved would have emphasised different aspects of the programme:

> "I think the ambition of Sure Start was to provide the opportunity to level up the children by recognising that if you start as early as you possibly can, you have the potential to deal with all of those issues that we know make a difference in education....

[T]here were some who felt very passionately that this was a very educationally focused exercise, that is was about, in a sense, providing early education much earlier ... there were others who thought it was much more about health and social care linked to education. There were those who thought it was much more about the community and that you specifically had Sure Start in areas where you were trying to build that sense of mothers and fathers coming together."

Not surprisingly, as she chaired the review, and was now a minister in both the DWP and DfES, Baroness Ashton supported the employability agenda. Indeed, she shared Morris's view that the Number 10 emphasis on education and the Number 11 emphasis on childcare for working parents could work together:

"The Treasury view was much more that this was about getting people into work, and the reason that that was so important as I recall, was that there was an absolute understanding that poverty cripples families and that working mothers, for all sorts of social, psychological and economic reasons, were able to provide more for their children."

Ashton is arguing that working mothers are good not only because they reduce child poverty, but also because employment itself is good for adult mental health. The well-being of mothers clearly must be good for their children.

What do we now mean by Sure Start?

Sure Start budget lines first appeared in April 1999. Barely three years later, the 2002 CSR created radical changes to the nature of the programme. By this time, about 300 SSLPs were actually up and running of the 500 announced in the previous CSR in 2000. The original programmes had been promised a 10-year life, with increasing funding for the first four years, then levelling off and decreasing over the last three years. All were still on an increasing funding trajectory, and were still finding it hard to get established and build buildings, so there was little resistance to the changes at this stage. Some preferred the label of 'Programme' rather than 'Centre', but, for most, aside from the childcare requirement, it was largely business as usual. For SSLPs, the change from the DH to DWP joint governance in Whitehall was barely noticed. But the increasing emphasis on childcare and working parents was uncomfortable and, in some areas, resisted. As already discussed in Chapter Four, childcare for working parents was not easy to combine with the very strong early emphasis on building capacity in local people, and improving their self-esteem and parenting skills. Like Blunkett and Jowell, SSLP managers were not opposed to childcare, they just did not think it was what Sure Start was all about.

The Childcare Review found that there were too many initiatives doing overlapping things with separate brands: Neighbourhood Nurseries, Early Excellence Centres, SSLPs and nursery education. There was a sense that Sure Start was a very valuable brand, and probably the most recognised of the four. Having looked at a range of new branding options, Catherine Ashton decided that all the activities under the new integrated Sure Start, Early Years and Childcare Unit would be covered under the name of Sure Start, with a newly designed and branded logo. But from this point on, what anyone thought was meant by Sure Start was increasingly complicated, particularly in that the childcare included care for school-aged children as well as under-fives. I shared the view that there was clear sense in developing greater alignment across early years and childcare policies. Fragmentation in Whitehall was not helping local implementation, but bringing it all together proved to be very challenging. Yet again there were competing sets of policy goals:

- services for all children under five to enhance educational outcomes for all;
- integrated services for poor children under four, with strong emphasis on parental support; and
- childcare for working parents for children from infancy to early teens.

Moreover, the cultures within the wide variety of agencies delivering the three policy goals were very different. The early education offer as envisioned in 1997 was a schools offer, delivered in nursery schools or in nursery classes attached to primary schools. Education institutions were largely about children, not about parents. The willingness of schools to engage with parents as partners was very variable. Childcare was usually a paid-for service, often delivered by the private sector. Parents were customers of a service that was meant to be flexible to accommodate their needs as employees. Childcare for school-aged children was even more complicated, pulling together the *extended schools* policies that up till then had largely been about after-school enrichment activities, and not explicitly about a paid-for service enabling parents to work. Integrated services for families in poverty had a strong culture of engaging parents, but the quality of services for children tended to be less good than in education settings. Services were largely designed to improve parenting skills and self-esteem usually for mothers. In the Sure Start integrated programmes, services for children were usually aligned to parent activities, either sessions that parents attended with their children or crèches organised while parents attended groups or courses. The focus was on improving child outcomes by improving parenting capacity and capabilities.

Aside from the tensions in the policy goals, funding strands for the different kinds of provision were complex. Ongoing arguments between supply-side funding and demand-side funding for childcare were unresolved. Should we give parents more cash in their pockets to purchase the childcare they want through increased childcare tax credits? Should we give suppliers in the poorest areas funding to ensure sustainability while demand built up? Or should all services be free?

Meanwhile, radical reform of all children's services: Every Child Matters

Chapter Two described the Labour government's commitment to new ways of policymaking and the commitment to children, in the first instance through education reform for all children. After the 1997 election, attention was turning to children growing up in poverty, including very young children, but also the impact of youth crime on poor neighbourhoods and the need to be tough on crime as well as on the causes of crime. *On Track* was a scheme set up to identify the children most likely to become offenders as early as age four and work with them and their families to change their predicted life course trajectory. Connexions had been established to bring together the careers service and the youth service into an integrated offer for young people aged 13 to 19 years old. The key concern was about young people who were 16 or older, post-compulsory school age and who were not in education, training or employment. There were two similarities with Sure Start: the principles of early intervention and service integration. The assumption was that by starting around age 13, you would be intervening early and thereby reducing the numbers who left school at 16 with no qualifications and no plans. Service integration was achieved by bringing together the careers service and the youth service. Moreover, the findings of the Childcare Review concerning the fragmentation of policy on childcare and early years education had resonance in the policy framework for all children across the age range from birth to 19. There was a multitude of initiatives and programmes all with their own inter-ministerial group, managed from different departments, with different local governance and delivery structures, and all claiming to be *joined up*. Indeed, every attempt to join up one policy area only resulted in fragmentation from others. The response to both the problems of joining up across Whitehall and joining up for disadvantaged children across the age range was the establishment of the Children and Young People's Unit (CYPU) and the Children's Fund.

The operational response to the lack of a specific programme for disadvantaged school-aged children was announced in the 2000 CSR, a new pot of money, the *Children's Fund*, would bridge the gap between Sure Start, On Track and Connexions. A ring-fenced pot of £450 million over three years was established to support local projects to help vulnerable children and young people aged eight to 13. There was a strong emphasis on using the voluntary sector, and a separate small portion of the money, the Local Network Fund, was dedicated to small local voluntary-sector projects.

The idea was a typical Whitehall solution: Sure Start for very young disadvantaged children, On Track and the Children's Fund to pick up the needs of disadvantaged children as they got older, and then on to Connexions for young people. On Track, Connexions and the Children's Fund had been established in part to tackle some of the challenges described in studies carried out by the Social Exclusion Unit, the unit set up in 1997 to solve the really wicked cross-cutting issues of deep disadvantage. However, differences in delivery mechanisms made joining up on the ground impossible. The Children's Fund was allocated to local authorities with the intention that they would commission services from the third sector; Sure Start was an area-based initiative, at this point still operating within very clear catchment areas for all children within particularly poor local wards; and Connexions was for all young people aged 13 to 19. So the idea of a seamless, inclusive service for disadvantaged children across the age range would not work given the differences in implementation of the three programmes. On the ground, programmes and, indeed, services for children would still be patchy and poorly coordinated.

Moreover, the Children's Fund did not solve the problem of coordination across Whitehall; it just added another initiative to be coordinated. The CYPU was established at the DfEE both to administer the Children's Fund and to coordinate across the whole of government the full range of policies affecting children and young people, from birth to 19. Like Sure Start, the CYPU had cross-government ministerial arrangements, in this case, between the Home Office and DfEE. David Blunkett at the DfEE and then Estelle Morris at the DfES represented the unit at cabinet, and Paul Boateng at the Home Office was the primary reporting minister for officials in the CYPU. The CYPU had its own cabinet committee officially chaired by the Chancellor, but in practice chaired by Boateng. Althea Efunshile was recruited to head up the new unit and took up post in January 2001, just months before the election in June. The CYPU identified three strands of work:

- Monitoring the impact of the new cross-Government guidance on local planning for children which aims to rationalize and improve the process for planning local services for children
- Leading the development of unified over-arching objectives for the delivery of services to children … and embedding these into policy making across all Government departments
- Developing an over-arching Government strategy for Children and Young People, focusing on the vulnerable but with a commitment to ensure coherence of approach for all. (CYPU, 2001a, p 31)

However, the twin tasks of administering a pot of money for a very diverse range of local activities for a particular age range of children suffering social exclusion while simultaneously coordinating and, to some extent, leading children's policy across government was enormously challenging, particularly as most of the key ministers changed within a few months of the establishment of the CYPU. After the election, David Blunkett moved to the Home Office, and he wanted to keep the cabinet responsibility, which now fell to Estelle Morris. John Denham replaced Paul Boateng at the Home Office and, as with any new minister, had different views on what the unit should be charged with doing. There were also differences of view between the Treasury and Number 10 on the role of the unit. The policy advisors at Number 10 were increasingly concerned with youth crime. The Treasury was taking the broader view set out in the Pre-Budget Report *Tackling Child Poverty*, described earlier in this chapter. Moreover, unlike Sure Start, children aged eight to 13 was not a *policy-free zone*. A very large number of Whitehall departments all claimed a stake, from health to education, from youth crime to drugs and alcohol; this was crowded territory with entrenched departmental cultures and interests.

Against these odds, the CYPU had some notable successes in addition to their contribution to the *Tackling Poverty* report. The unit was pushing very hard for policies concerning children and young people to be designed with them as active participants in the process. A green paper was produced, *Tomorrow's Future* (CYPU, 2001a), which began some serious thinking about how children and young people's services could be based more clearly on the views of children and young people themselves. At the time I had concerns that an emphasis on child participation would yet again leave out the youngest children; consulting with under-fours did not seem feasible. I also felt that there needed to be at least some ideas about involving parents. Engaging with parents was important for two reasons: first, without them the needs of the very youngest children would not be understood from a user rather than a provider perspective; and, second, the views of parents and children could differ and it was important to recognise the inherent tensions possible in a *user-led* approach that was unclear about who the user was. Certainly, within the DfES at the time, the user was the parent with increasing rights to school choice. For the CYPU it was definitely the child or young person.

The second major contribution of the CYPU was an intensive piece of work led by John Rowlands on designing a core set of *outcomes* against which all children's services should be judged. Aligned with the principles just outlined, these outcomes were largely derived from intensive participation activities with children and young people. Sure Start also had an emphasis on outcomes, as reflected in some of its initial Public Service Agreement (PSA) targets. However, the Sure Start outcomes were derived at the centre of government in consultation with professionals and academics. It was then up to users with local professionals to determine how at local level these outcomes should be delivered. The CYPU approach was to develop the outcomes framework with children and young people themselves, as well as parents, professionals and academics. This was a radical step and one that had significant impact on the major changes to children's services ahead. The work on a group of core principles to guide children's services and an initial group of outcomes was set out in a consultation paper published by the CYPU in November 2001. Three of the five outcomes that were eventually to be enshrined in the Every Child Matters (ECM) agenda were set out in this paper. Children themselves identified the following as most important for them: 'Health and Well being, Achievement and Enjoyment, and Participation and Citizenship' (CYPU, 2001b, p 18).

Events drive the agenda

As is often the case, an individual high-profile tragedy became the critical stimulus for change. Victoria Climbié was an eight-year-old child who died of severe physical abuse and neglect at the hands of her aunt and her aunt's boyfriend. Particularly shocking in the Climbié case was the number of different agencies that had been in contact with her and failed to recognise the severity of her situation. This child's death gave new urgency to the need to reform the systems supporting particularly vulnerable children and families. Central to the findings of Lord Laming's published report into the death were features that had been part of many of the previous tragedies involving child deaths:

- a failure to intervene when problems first come to the attention of public services;
- poor co-ordination across services;
- the absence of clear accountability at local level; and
- poor staff management and training (see HMG, 2003).

At the same time, the Prime Minister had asked John Birt, previously Director General of the BBC, to review the state of services related to youth crime, and in particular the prevention of youth criminality. Both the Laming report and Birt's unpublished report came to similar conclusions about a broken system that was uncoordinated, ineffective, putting children and young people at risk, and not making best use of public money. They did not, however, come up with similar recommendations. Birt was viewing the problem through a prism of anti-social behaviour, while Laming was seeking to protect vulnerable children. Indeed, this tension between children as the cause of social problems or as the victims of social ills was reflected in many of the policies and programmes coming from Whitehall. Birt's view was that local government was not up to the task of preventing youth crime. He proposed a new national service to deal with young offenders and potential offenders. Laming held the view that the system to protect children needed radical reform, but the fundamental basis of delivery through social workers based in local authorities should not change.

While the relatively young CYPU was working intensively on issues of defining the right set of outcomes and engaging young people in their deliberations, the Prime Minister asked his Strategy Unit to conduct a root-and-branch review of children's services. The team, led by Ravi Gurumurthy, was based at the Cabinet Office to ensure that no individual departmental interest would dominate the analysis or the conclusions. The result was the ECM green paper published in the Autumn of 2003. Among the most significant changes for Whitehall were:

- the disbanding of the CYPU and the creation of a higher-level directorate within the DfES, the Children, Young People and Families Directorate;
- the responsibility for social care for children, along with teenage pregnancy, family policy, and family law, being moved from the DH and Home Office to the DfES;
- the creation of a new Minister of State role, the Children's Minister, with no other responsibilities but children's policy; and
- the proposal to establish a Children's Commissioner post for England.

Given the range of policy responsibilities now within the DfES, it became clear that the wide breadth of children's issues within the department would need a Director General-level lead of a much larger group of civil servants than was envisioned with the CYPU. The work started by CYPU on an outcomes framework became a key feature in the ECM green paper. In addition to the three outcomes of health, achievement and participation identified earlier, economic well-being and staying safe completed the set of five outcomes that quickly became visible in virtually every agency that works with children in England. The two added outcomes are not surprising: staying safe was clearly a response to Victoria Climbié, and economic well-being tied in with the key aim of ending child poverty. This green paper and the eventual legislation that followed it in 2004 fundamentally changed the way most professionals concerned with children in England think about their work. Hopefully, it also changed the way most of them do their work. Working in silos without thinking about the role other services play in determining child outcomes would no longer be acceptable. Accountability at local level would be clear and unambiguous, and accountability would be for *children*, not just for education or social care. Services would be designed around the needs of the child and family, not narrowly defined professional interests.

Besides the critically important outcomes framework, the green paper set out an ambitious set of reforms including:

- the need for improved information-sharing;
- the need for a common assessment framework across all professionals working with children and families;

- the development of the lead professional role, to hold the ring and ensure the delivery of a coherent set of services for children with multiple needs;
- the creation of Directors of Children's Services and Lead Council Members, responsible for all children's services in the local authority area;
- the creation of Children's Trust Boards to ensure partnership arrangements are in place with all those critically involved in children's services locally, local government, schools, health, police, and the third sector; and
- the creation of Local Safeguarding Children's Boards (HMG, 2003, p 7)

It was recognised that significant changes needed to be made to the children's workforce to make this happen, including agreeing that anyone working with children needed to have a core set of knowledge and skills, and that work needed to be done to establish precisely what should be in such a core set.

Many of the issues identified across the system in the ECM green paper had been causing real problems for Sure Start. Clearly, work on creating more effective inter-agency partnerships would be a help, as would improvements in information-sharing. Both of these had proved really difficult for SSLP managers who often did not have support at a senior enough level in either health or the local authority to bring services together. The creation of Directors of Children's Services was intended to ensure that there would be one very senior person with responsibility for the full range of children's services within each local authority. This proved to be a mixed blessing. As will be explored in Chapter Seven, there were dangers ahead. Up to this point, local Sure Start programme managers had a very high degree of independence, and generally thought of their line management coming from the Sure Start Boards, which always included local parents, and from Whitehall, a long distance away. If local authorities and, indeed, Directors of Children's Services were to have a much clearer line of accountability for all children in the patch, this had to include Sure Start. Loss of neighbourhood control was coming, and was not welcomed by many local Sure Start managers or, indeed, some local parents. What was started with the 2002 Childcare Review's recommendation of a bigger role for local authorities was becoming more real, and was beginning to threaten the principle of community control so fundamental to the original basis of Sure Start.

Who says government is slow?

When viewed retrospectively, the changes in policies affecting children in the first few years of the Labour government were astounding, both in terms of resource allocation for new programmes and the seniority and number of civil servants working on children's issues across Whitehall. When I started working in the DfEE in 1999, the Sure Start Unit fell within the management of a group at the DfEE called the Pupil, School and Inclusion Group. This group was managed within what was then the Schools Directorate, with the Director General of Schools on the DfEE board reporting to the Permanent Secretary. There was no board-level post concerning children and families. All issues concerning children that were outside the universal provision of education for children from five to 16 fell into this relatively small group: special educational needs, behaviour and truancy, early education and so on. Indeed, it was rare to hear anyone in the department talk about children; they usually talked about pupils and teachers. Childcare was a means to an end, that is, lone-parent employment.

By 2007, the DfEE had become the Department for *Children*, Schools and *Families*, with a Director General leading a significantly larger cadre of civil servants on policy to do with children's social care, safeguarding, early years, childcare, information-sharing, change implementation at local authority level and special needs. The policy development that led to these really radical changes happened over a relatively few years, and over a number of changes of ministers, but the direction of travel was clear; the DfEE was moving from a department that was about schools and teachers to a department that was about the widest possible range of issues affecting children. Some of these changes reflected early practice in SSLPs, and some of the changes were instrumental in improving what Sure Start could achieve. It is highly likely that the receptiveness of local authorities to the changes was helped by their Sure Start experience. All children, not just the very young and the very poor, needed joined-up services that were about the whole child: their health, social well-being and educational attainment. Given the change of government in May 2010, the sustainability of these reforms is yet to be seen. The rapidness with which the Department for Children, Schools and Families became the Department for Education was greeted by many in the children's policy world with concern.

Chapter Seven will explore in more detail the implications this had for Sure Start as it moved from an innovative programme engaging local communities in delivering a diverse range of services for young children and their parents, to a considerably more standardised national offer for all families, building a new and permanent feature of the welfare state.

Sure Start grows up

This part of the Sure Start story describes its change from a time-limited initiative to a permanent part of the welfare state, what in law every parent has a right to expect in their local neighbourhood for their young children. This chapter will tell three key stories in the development of Sure Start:

- the impact on Sure Start Local Programmes (SSLPs) of the merger at the Department for Education and Skills (DfES) of Sure Start, Early Years Education and Childcare, and particularly the impact of the 2002 Comprehensive Spending Review (CSR);
- the development of *Choice for Parents, the Best Start for Children: A Ten Year Strategy for Childcare,* the document produced by the Treasury and DfES that set the framework for early years and childcare services for the foreseeable future; and
- the launch of the Ten Year Strategy and the media uproar following the publication, which heralded the end of Sure Start.

The backdrop of these three strands is the development of the Every Child Matters (ECM) agenda. As the DfES took over responsibility for more and more aspects of policy concerning children, keeping Sure Start separate and special became increasingly untenable. What started out as key delivery aims for children under four – joined-up services designed flexibly to deliver improved outcomes for young children – increasingly became the aims for all children. The framework for all children, the ECM agenda, had to include the youngest and the poorest children. The 2002 and 2004 CSRs were moving Sure Start inexorably from a specialist, ring-fenced cross-departmental *initiative* to the mainstream of children's services.

While the Childcare Review in 2002 started this journey, the publication of a major report, *Choice for Parents, the Best Start for Children: A Ten Year Strategy for Childcare* (HMT, 2004) committed the government to the end destination. The implications for what were SSLPs were greeted with dismay by some and enthusiasm by others. Certainly, the Sure Start experience as an innovative initiative with time-limited funding was drawing to a close. SSLPs, all now Children's Centres, were to be integrated into a comprehensive service for all children and families. Three streams of work were identified at the end of Chapter Three: early education for all children; childcare for working parents; and integrated services for poor children. The Ten Year Strategy would bring all of these together to form a coherent offer for children before school age.

For some time during this period, Sure Start fell out of favour. Press reports about the loss of local control along with disappointing evaluation results began to tarnish the once-shining brand. Oddly, the two stories argued diametrically opposing positions; loss of local control was mourned as the death of the programme, but the evaluation results pushed for considerably more control from the centre. It seemed to some that by letting a thousand flowers bloom, we had cultivated a number of weeds. Detailed discussion of the evaluation results and government's response to them will come in Chapter Eight.

The period from 2003 to 2006 also saw several changes of ministers, both at Minister of State and Secretary of State level and in both of the two key departments of Sure Start governance, the Department for Work and Pensions (DWP) and the DfES. Charles Clarke, who had taken over as Secretary of State at the DfES from Estelle Morris in the autumn of 2002, left at the end of 2004 to run the Home Office. Clarke was replaced by Ruth Kelly. Baroness Ashton left the DfES a few months before Charles Clarke, in September 2004, to be replaced by Lord Filkin. Andrew Smith had replaced Alistair Darling at the DWP in 2002. There were more changes after the spring election in 2005; Margaret Hodge moved to the Department of Culture, Media and Sport, and was replaced by Beverley Hughes as Minister for Children. David Blunkett replaced Andrew Smith as Secretary of State at the DWP. Ruth Kelly left the DfES in 2006, and was replaced by Alan Johnson. Each one of these ministers was different not only in style, but also very often in substance. Finally, as described in Chapter Six, it was a very turbulent time for children's services more generally, with the huge structural changes heralded by the ECM agenda beginning to take hold.

Another spending review, another Public Service Agreement

The 2002 CSR revised again the main aim of Sure Start and its Public Service Agreement (PSA) targets. The main aim is reproduced as follows, with the change in the aim from the 2000 CSR in italics:

Increase the availability of childcare for all children, and work with parents to be, parents and children to promote the physical, intellectual and social development of babies and young children – particularly those who are disadvantaged – so that they can flourish at home and at school, *enabling their parents to work and contributing to the ending of child poverty*. (HMT, 2002, p 43)

There were two critical changes in the aim: the ambition to increase childcare for children of all ages and the explicit reference to the goal of ending child poverty. The previous aims statements from 1998 and 2000 were about ameliorating the effects of poverty on low-income children in the current generation so as to break the cycle of intergenerational poverty. We were now in the territory of not only ensuring that the current generation of children are not poor as adults, but attempting to reduce current levels of child poverty through reducing the number of children living in workless households. There is no doubt that this was a huge issue in Sure Start areas. On average, nearly half of children under four in Sure Start areas were living in workless households (Barnes, 2007, p 31). The 2002 CSR brought together two key policy goals for the Labour government that had been evident since 1998: reducing child poverty and improving longer-term outcomes for disadvantaged children. The specific PSA targets linked to the aims were broadly similar to those of 2000.

Measuring the PSA targets was an ongoing problem. Success in meeting the targets that could be measured continued to be very slow, and the reliability of the data for others was very poor. We simply did not have the infrastructure to collect reliable information on eminently desirable outcomes like smoking in pregnancy in the Sure Start programme catchment areas. The agreement that some of the SSLP services like childcare would now be available for families outside the specific catchment areas made data collection and analysis even more difficult. Clearly, we wanted to encourage women not to smoke whether they lived in the catchment area or not. But would an individual who gave up smoking but lived in another area count towards the target? In retrospect, these may seem like silly arguments, but these were new processes that we really wanted to make work. Funding for outcomes rather than inputs was a key principle of Sure Start from the very beginning. We did not anticipate how fiendishly complicated it would be.

Furthermore, as was mentioned in Chapter Three, the overlap of CSR periods meant that, at any one time, SSLPs were trying to address two different sets of PSA targets while their main efforts were in getting programmes established. The targets were meant for *fully operational programmes*, and it was taking around three years for programmes to be fully operational (Meadows, 2007, p 121). Our original aim was for 250 programmes to be established by 2002 and then 500 programmes to be established by 2004. By June 2000, only 59 programmes had approved plans, which meant they could recruit staff and receive revenue (Melhuish and Hall, 2007, p 14). In the 2002 CSR, we were changing the fundamental nature of what an SSLP was meant to be when fewer than half of the 500 programmes were approved, let alone close to being fully operational.

The basic idea of a Sure Start programme continued to be a locally based centre with facilities for health, early education and play, parenting advice and support, and childcare. But, in addition, there would also be information, advice and encouragement towards employment. The Sure Start strapline on all the information and literature became:

> Sure Start aims to achieve better outcomes for children, parents and communities by:
> - Increasing the availability of childcare for all children
> - Improving the health education and emotional development for young children
> - Supporting parents as parents and in their aspirations towards employment. (DfES, 2002, p 7)

Estelle Morris resigned as Secretary of State at the DfES in the autumn of 2002. She was replaced by Charles Clarke. In preparing a brief on early years and childcare for the new Secretary of State, we established a new narrative: what government was offering all children – nursery education and childcare; and what government was offering poor children – SSLPs/Children's Centres. At this stage, Sure Start still meant integrated services targeted in areas of deprivation, but now with the joint aim of reducing child poverty and improving the life course trajectories of poor children. The Sure Start Children's Centres described in the 2002 Childcare Review replaced the SSLPs, and were the main service strategy for addressing poverty in families with young children. Eventually, the Sure Start Children's Centre offer became an offer for all children and families, but that was yet to come. At that time, the challenge was making the childcare offer work for the wider age range of children, up to 13 instead of up to four, while greatly expanding the number of Children's Centres and increasing what they offered.

Childcare for all: under-fives

The inclusion of childcare for all children in the Sure Start aim reflected the integration of the Sure Start Unit with the Early Years and Childcare Unit at the DfES described in Chapter Six. At this point, we were well on the way to fulfilling the commitment of free early education for all three- and four-year-olds. Encouraging much closer working between the Neighbourhood Nursery Initiative (NNI) and Sure Start was eminently sensible. NNI was set up to ensure that there was an adequate provision of childcare in poor areas for working parents. Given the difficulty of establishing childcare businesses, the NNI would provide a revenue stream that would reduce over three years while numbers built up in new nurseries. It made sense to use some of the capital funding for what were SSLPs for childcare provision. Putting both benefits advice and employment services in Sure Start Centres also made sense. Indeed, many SSLPs had already included benefits advice and some even had credit unions on the premises. The fundamental idea was that parents who came to a centre for any number of reasons, including just social support with other mothers and fathers, would, through engagement, be encouraged to consider taking up paid employment, or the kind of training that could lead to employment. The key was for the parents who were most likely to be on benefits to see the childcare on the premises and be reassured that care was available should they find employment. The benefits advice would reassure them that they would actually be better off working some number of hours per week, even with childcare costs, than if they remained unemployed. Indeed, in many of the centres the childcare was heavily subsidised.

However, for some centres the childcare offer proved difficult for a number of reasons. Some of the earliest programmes simply had not made any provision for childcare in their capital development. Many later programmes did their capital development linked to primary schools, which already offered *free* nursery education. The pattern in many of these centres was to have the children in the school for their free 2.5 hours a day, and then move them to the Children's Centre for their *wrap-around* childcare, paid for by parents. Bizarrely, this sometimes meant childcare on one side of a corridor in a school building and nursery education on the other side, with different staffing and sometimes different management arrangements. Sometimes this resulted in greatly improved joint working between the school and the Children's Centre, but at other times it continued to be fragmented. So much of what has been learned about the difficulties of joined-up services was evident in the variety of arrangements made for integration of the early education offer, basically through schools, and the childcare offer, usually through the private or voluntary sector. It was mainly in the Early Excellence Centres that real integration between care and education was happening. Real integration meant the high quality associated with teacher–led early learning in a childcare setting offering flexible hours for working parents. After all, the child's needs do not change depending on who is managing or working in the provision. However, if it proved too difficult to offer this kind of ideal integration, many parents wanted to ensure that their child got some experience of settings with highly trained teachers for part of the day, even if it meant moving to what was likely to be a lower-quality setting for the other part of the day. The key was ensuring at least 2.5 hours a day of *early education*. These very difficult issues were to emerge again in the key debates in developing the Ten Year Strategy described later in this chapter.

Key barriers to integration included a schools culture that was often inflexible about offering different patterns of attendance suitable for working parents, and a schools culture that was reluctant to charge fees for additional hours beyond the free entitlement of 12.5 hours per week delivered over five days per week. Some teachers saw childcare as little more than babysitting. Given that early years education was, and still is, the lowest status area of the education world, combining it with childcare only reinforced the notion that this was basic work that anyone could do. Nursery teachers were particularly reluctant to do anything that blurred the distinction between childcare and education as it would weaken the already low status of teaching very young children.

Moreover, the overarching aim of increasing employment was also problematic. There was little point in encouraging the provision of new childcare places if local parents were not encouraged to seek paid work. While some programmes embraced this agenda, many others were deeply resistant. There continued to be a view that women with small children should not work. Evidence on whether childcare was good or damaging for children continued to be accumulated by the warring camps. Jane Waldfogel reviewed all the evidence in detail and concluded:

> Two findings particularly stand out. One, children whose mothers work in the first year of life, particularly if they work full time, do tend to have lower cognitive test scores at age three and thereafter.... Two, we have learned something about how these effects come about. Some of the adverse

effects of early maternal employment on later cognitive outcomes are due to children receiving poorer-quality child care or less sensitive care at home. But if maternal employment raises family incomes, there are positive effects on children's cognitive development. (Waldfogel, 2006, p 55)

So the evidence supported the view that there were some risks in childcare for children under one year old, but that poverty reduction was good for children. Despite this, some Sure Start staff remained uncomfortable with the employment agenda:

While some Sure Start local programmes see encouraging parents to find paid work as a central part of their objective of improving the well-being of children and families, others perceive a tension between encouraging parents to go out to work and supporting the belief of many parents that part of being a good parent is to be at home with children when they are young. (Meadows and Garbers, 2004, p 3)

Recalling my own experience of working at the front line, I have a personal view on the resistance of many staff to the employment agenda. Many of the staff working in SSLPs positively enjoyed the work with adults: running groups, setting up drop-in sessions, engaging parents in a wide range of community activities and so on. Working parents would not be available to attend the baby massage session on Tuesday afternoon, or the cooking class on Wednesday morning. In many discussions with the people who worked directly with parents, they expressed concern that the (mainly) women who came to the centres did not want jobs. I think, to some extent, those working with such women were content to build their self-esteem, raise their confidence and continue to enjoy what often were very warm relationships until the children were of school age. The more women went to work, the fewer would be available to attend the groups and sessions run in the Children's Centres. As reported in earlier chapters, ministers themselves had different views on the importance of childcare and encouraging employment in Sure Start Centres. Yvette Cooper commented in the interview for this book:

"I remember getting frustrated when Sure Start Centres were set up and didn't have childcare in ... for some of the early programmes it felt like a massive missed opportunity and that parents would be more likely to use the childcare if it was also in a centre they were used to going to for drop-ins and other informal services."

As already mentioned in Chapter Four, both David Blunkett and Tessa Jowell were uncomfortable about childcare, Jowell because her focus was on babies and mothers, and Blunkett because his key focus was precisely the kind of community engagement that staff in the centres thought they should be doing. Margaret Hodge had as her main concern the quality of the early education experience for the child. As a champion of Early Excellence Centres, she worked hard to get this aligned with a childcare agenda, but her heart was in education. As we will see later in the chapter, Beverley Hughes was principally concerned with the quality of parent support and the quality of experience for the child. While she supported the childcare agenda, she was concerned that if staff were going to spend time on running groups for parents, they should be using structured programmes that had some evidence of effectiveness. Even from the very centre of government, there were differences of view. The Chancellor was strongly committed to childcare as a welfare-to-work strategy, and the Prime Minister had some concerns about childcare for very young children. Indeed, he was considering some European models where the mother is paid to stay at home with her children for as long as three years.

Childcare for all: school-aged children

Now that Sure Start was meant to deliver childcare for all, the challenge for school-aged children was just as daunting. The barriers with older children were also largely to do with the culture of schools. Yet again, a new policy brings to the surface tensions in policies that have considerable common features, but some inherent difficulties in both philosophical and practical applications. The task was to join up an emerging strategy called *Extended Schools* with the aim to deliver school-based childcare. The development of Extended Schools in England dated back to a Social Exclusion Unit report in 1998 (Social Exclusion Unit, 1998). The basic idea was that schools should be a community resource that would house a range of activities beyond the school day, and beyond the narrow teaching and learning activities in traditional schools. Some of these additional activities would themselves enhance educational outcomes, but others would be concerned with health, sport or access to wider services for local people, not just pupils attending the schools:

Starting in 2002, the Department for Education and Skills (DFES) began to actively promote the concept of 'extended schools'. They did this initially through some demonstration projects and then by sponsoring twenty five local education authorities (LEAs) to develop extended schools pathfinder projects. Each project was free to determine the focus of its work, though particular encouragement was offered to initiatives that would lead to:

- Schools that are open to pupils, families and the wider community during and beyond the school day, before and after school hours, at weekends and during school holidays;
- Activities aimed particularly at vulnerable groups, in areas of deprivation and/or where services are limited;
- The promotion of community cohesion by building links between schools and the wider community;
- The provision of services to communities;
- A contribution to neighbourhood renewal; and
- A positive effect on educational standards. (Smith, 2004, 2005, pp 3–4)

The Extended School programme looks very like the original Sure Start programme model, although clearly built on a solid schools infrastructure. Each of the demonstration projects mentioned above would have the freedom to determine what would be appropriate locally, and there is a similar emphasis on ameliorating disadvantage. The list of possible aims is very broad indeed, and evaluation of the programme would therefore prove to be problematic. The list of possible services to be co-located in schools does look very much like Sure Start programmes: health and health promotion, adult education, employment training and jobs advice, family welfare services, childcare and so on (Smith, 2004, 2005, pp 3–4). But the key problem with the Extended Schools programme and childcare was the issue of charging. Some head teachers were not happy about multiple service provision in schools at all. Others could see the benefits, and a small number had been opening up their schools for outside groups and agencies for years. Voluntary organisations had been running activities out of school hours in schools and in local areas linked to schools for some time. But head teachers and, indeed, governing bodies had great difficulty with charging. There were complex legal restrictions on charging, particularly on activities that were directly supportive of educational attainment. The rationale for not charging was obvious and quite sensible; it would be wrong to charge for extra support for learning that would most likely benefit the children from the poorest families. While the tax credit system was meant to ensure that childcare was affordable, distinguishing between what was charged for and what was not was complicated.

There were two related problems: childcare was a service that parents paid for, and after-school activities were often irregular. The difficulty that Catherine Ashton and I mulled over for months was how to bring together study support, after-school sports and leisure with childcare. Children who attended anything but childcare were rarely charged, except occasional fees for equipment or outings. Schools were very uncomfortable about services for which parents paid fees. Furthermore, the school staff who supervised the after-school activities considered that the children participated voluntarily. Hence, the second problem was the unreliability of after-school activities. If the teacher who ran the maths club was off sick, the children who attended the club were sent home. The club was free, the day it was run could change from term to term and, on occasion, it may not happen at all. These arrangements would not work, even for a parent who wanted to work part time. Working parents needed to know that alternative care arrangements would be in place if the maths club did not happen.

What seemed particularly perverse was that the law allowed for the charging of activities that were not related to educational achievement, but did not allow for charging if it did. Children whose parents worked and who were young enough to still need childcare could not go to the maths club because it simply would not be a reliable or regular enough service for a working parent. A series of complex changes to regulations and new legislation eventually sorted out many of these difficulties. The key point is that particular services and programmes emerged from different histories. The needs of the eight-year-old are not that complicated. The needs of the eight-year-old seen through the eyes of a teacher, a youth worker or, indeed, a lone mother wanting to get paid work are going to be described differently and be organised from the history and culture of the service provider, not the service user. Furthermore, in the case of most children's services, the needs of the child service user do not always coincide with the needs of the parent as service user. It is easy to return to the principles again of Modernising Government: joining up services, user- not provider-led, driven by local context and so on. Making those principles apply to suit the needs of diverse families, working or not working, wanting the maths club or wanting to chill out in front of the TV, with changing patterns within families and across communities, turned out to be really difficult.

While Sure Start programmes were building up their service structure, moving to a more defined Children's Centre model and coping with increasing pressure to develop childcare and employment services, the task of bringing together Extended Schools and childcare for school-aged children was complex both in policy development and in implementation. The cultural resistance in many schools was a powerful barrier. Moreover, childcare in schools felt like another distraction from the main business. The government had spent the first few years following 1997 intensely focusing on educational attainment. Would developing childcare and other extended services from schools result in taking the eye off the ball in terms of the key task of improving test results?

Number 10 gets worried

In many ways, Extended Schools seemed like Sure Start up the age range. There was increasing momentum for an all-children, all-age service offer that included greatly improved school performance, a wider offer of childcare for younger children, before- and after-school services for over-fives, and a range of support and community services delivered from pre-school settings and from schools. Much of this thinking had already been developed in the Childcare Review of 2002. It was also consistent with the thinking of the ECM agenda, a clear and progressive offer for all children that was sensitive to any specific needs of disadvantaged children. However, although progress was being made, it was not quick enough for key staff in Number 10. Furthermore, there was increasing concern that we did not seem to have a clear trajectory for getting to where we needed to be or, indeed, a clear idea of what the destination looked like. Two very different events generated concern at Number 10, one rather ad hoc and the other quite formal.

The ad hoc event started with a leaflet delivered to Andrew Adonis. In 2002, Adonis, now Lord Adonis, was leading on education in the Policy Unit at Number 10. Adonis lived in London and had young children. He received a leaflet through his front door inviting his family to use the SSLP. Among the activities listed was *aromatherapy*. This caused great consternation on two fronts. Sure Start was meant for disadvantaged families. Why was the SSLP trying to involve his family? But, more importantly for Adonis, why aromatherapy? Clearly there was no evidence that such activities improve child outcomes. Given all the early promises of Sure Start as the means to cure all the ill effects of growing up in poverty, why was the government providing benign but ineffective activities for people who probably do not need them. Carey Oppenheim, who was then advisor responsible for childcare and social security, got the full force of his anger and rang me in a panic. Her recent comments reflect the dilemmas we faced:

> "We were obviously then in an argument about how do you engage people and keep them coming in? But I think that was a genuine issue and, of course, now in terms of the guidance, it's moving more towards setting very strong expectations in relation to the kind of outcomes that have to be achieved, and in terms of what kinds of parenting support is most effective. But I think that took quite a while to sort out."

There were answers to both of these questions. We knew that an area-based initiative would involve all the families in the area, not just those on benefit. In London, where within very small geographical areas the rich and poor live side by side, it was bound to happen that Sure Start would attract not only poor families, but all families. This perception and resulting criticism of Sure Start being used by too many families, who were not poor enough, will be explored in more detail in Chapter Eight when we discuss the evaluation results.

The second issue, providing activities that are not evidenced-based, is a bit trickier. The early emphasis in Sure Start on engaging local service users in determining what should be on offer was still a very strong driver in SSLPs. If a significant number of mainly mothers wanted aromatherapy, then it was consistent with the ethos of Sure Start to offer it. But the tension remains between user-driven services and services with a clear evidence base for effectiveness. The tension also remains between local or national design. When Beverley Hughes became Minister for Children in 2005, she had similar concerns to those raised by Adonis some years earlier: who was Sure Start for and what should it be doing?

> "I was going around Children's Centres in the early days and there was a lack of focus in some places on really identifying the families that needed most help and the children that needed the most help, and focusing also on the quality of the early education and child development aspect.

I was very keen that parents should be involved, but I think I began to feel that there needed to be a greater consensus around what Children's Centres were there for, and a movement towards at least providing a core minimum about what was available and to a minimum standard, and that other things could be built around that."

Hughes was seeking a similarly rigorous approach to the work with parents:

"There were some places where people were being trained in a very sensitive way to use one of the validated programmes, and really clear that that was necessary to get benefits. There were other places where when you asked what they were doing, they said they devised their own programmes and they could not answer the key question about impact. They were allowed to do their own thing really in a way that was very uncritical and not validated."

Again, these issues will be explored in Chapter Eight on the evaluation results and in the final chapter on what we have learned. Suffice it to say here that we have learned that local people do not often ask for the latest evidenced-based *intervention* in the same way that they do not always ask for help with finding employment. It takes very skilled staff to negotiate what the current users of a Sure Start Centre say they want, what research evidence says they need and what behaviours the government wants to see. Using aromatherapy to develop engagement with users can be a helpful tactic only if it is followed by a clear plan of action to work with mothers and fathers on other activities that have more explicit benefits for children. Conversely, offering a range of evidence-based programmes that mothers and fathers are not keen to take up will not improve outcomes for children. If the current government's ideas for the Big Society become realised, these tensions will continue to be played out between what people articulate as their needs, and what evidence tells us works to improve outcomes for their children.

The second specific event that raised early concerns about progress was a meeting with the Prime Minister in January 2003. The Prime Minister held regular 'stock takes' with key delivery departments – Health, the Home Office and Education. These events, largely stage-managed by the Prime Minister's Delivery Unit (PMDU), were designed to give reassurance to the Prime Minister that his key delivery goals were on track. They were attended by the relevant Secretary of State, the Permanent Secretary and a small group of senior officials from the department. I am not sure why, but Sure Start was added to the agenda of the DfES for the early 2003 meeting. On the schools side, data was extremely well presented. Michael Barber, who headed up the PMDU, had previously been at the DfES and had set up much of the system for data collection and analysis on schools performance. He did an excellent short, sharp summary of where we were on attainment, where we needed to be and, most importantly, the plans to get there. On the early years side, we simply did not have the sophisticated systems in place, and many of the key data sets were in the process of being set up. Having recently read Barber's book, *Instructions to Deliver* (Barber, 2007, p 95), I realise now how we got such an important meeting wrong. Baroness Ashton and I were jointly presenting, but neither of us anticipated the detail of the questions that the PM would be asking. We thought we had a good story to tell, but it was not the story he wanted to hear. While having the opportunity to present to the Prime Minister was tremendously exciting, my preparation should have been much better. Barber makes this point more generally for the civil service in his book. He is surprised at the inability of many civil servants to present clear information quickly and succinctly. For this meeting, the Prime Minister wanted to know how many Children's Centres there would be altogether, and how many would be set up by when. Our problem was that we were still debating what level of services would be required to set up a Children's Centre, so had no idea how much each Centre would cost to run. We knew that there would be more than the 500 SSLPs, but depending on whether a Children's Centre costs £150,000 per year or £500,000 per year would determine how many could be established. Charles Clarke was interested in a scaled-down approach, a kind of *Sure Start lite*, but no detailed costings had been made, nor the important policy decisions on precisely what a Children's Centre needed to be. We could not answer the Prime Minister's questions.

It was a scarring experience and one that left a feeling of unease at Number 10 about our progress. Furthermore, we were short on quick wins. The government liked having new things to announce. Given the size and complexity of the already announced commitments, and the time it was taking to get all the various components going, it was hard to find something new to say, and results were not yet coming through on the complex Sure Start evaluation. The Number 10 Policy Unit was also concerned that the ambitions on childcare were not keeping pace with what would be needed if employment and anti-poverty targets were to be met. Hence, it was decided early in 2004 to bring all the policies together under a single framework, a document that would combine all early years services including Sure Start and out-of-school-hours childcare into a single strategy.

Choice for Parents, the Best Start for Children: A Ten Year Strategy for Childcare – a second go at bringing it all together

It is unclear where the idea for a new strategy emerged. In interviews for this book with some of the key players, no one remembered who thought it up. It was developed over a year, one of the most difficult years of my working life, but, in my view, the end result still stands as a remarkable achievement that has indeed set the framework and forward momentum for early years services. It was also an intensely creative policy process, driven between the Treasury, the Number 10 Policy Unit and the DfES. The key player at Number 10 was Carey Oppenheim, at the Treasury it was the Chancellor's Chief of Staff, Ed Miliband, and at the DfES it was Charles Clarke's senior advisor, Robert Hill. On the civil service side, the DfES leads were Ann Gross and Linda Uren, both of whom worked for me, but, for this project, worked mainly for Robert Hill. Key officials at the Treasury were Ray Shostak, Stephen Meek and Ann Taggart (now Watt). The DWP and the then Department of Trade and Industry were also involved, but to a much lesser extent than the Treasury, Number 10 and the DfES. The final document, *Choice for Parents, the Best Start for Children: a Ten Year Strategy for Childcare* was published as a Pre-Budget Report (PBR) document on 4 December 2004 (HMT, 2004).

There is actually very little in the document about Sure Start. Indeed, we had a debate on whether to drop the Sure Start brand altogether. Schools and hospitals are not branded. Everyone knows what they are for. We were creating a similar set of expectations and commitments for younger children. We hoped that, eventually, the commitments set out in the strategy would come to be seen as normal a part of what the state offers its citizens as schools and health care. The real issue was what role did the Sure Start Children's Centre model play in an integrated all-children service offer? The decision was taken to keep the name Sure Start for Children's Centres only, going back on the decision taken by Baroness Ashton in 2002 to call all the early years and childcare services Sure Start. From now on, and as of this writing, Sure Start is used for Children's Centres only, as part of a much broader set of entitlements for under-fives and school-aged children that are now enshrined in law. As will be described at the end of this chapter, for some, this was the death of Sure Start. The key debates in developing the strategy brought to the surface many of the tensions in childcare policy that had not been properly aired. There were some very serious decisions to make, and strong disagreements between key players among and between politicians and officials. The differences of view were often deeply held convictions about what would be best for children; they did not fall neatly into departmental interests. And, for the first time, the strategy included not only plans for childcare, but changes to the childcare element of the Working Tax Credit, changes to paid maternity leave and commitments to improving paternity leave. As the title implies, the strategy was not just about childcare, it was also about improving that very elusive aim of balancing work and family life.

The key debates

The government's stated vision for the strategy was: 'to ensure that every child gets the best start in life and to give parents more choice about how to balance work and family live' (HMT, 2004, p 1). Four key issues needed to be addressed to realise the vision: choice and flexibility for parents; availability of childcare for all up to the age of 14; quality of childcare; and affordability. Each of these involved intense negotiation, argument and compromise. As will be described later, some were not quite mutually exclusive, but were in tension with one another. No matter how hard we tried, not everyone could have everything.

There were two key arguments for 'choice and flexibility': maternity leave and flexible use of hours. On maternity leave, evidence was accumulating that, particularly in the first 12 months, there were some risks to group childcare (Sylva, 2010b, p 226). In 1997, paid maternity leave was just 18 weeks. This had been increased by the government to 26 weeks paid leave, with the option of returning to work after 12 months, that is, half-year paid, and half-year unpaid, maternity leave. The Scandinavian experience was that women, particularly lower-paid women, would only take the paid leave, and not the unpaid leave. As paid leave was increased, so did the number of women who were choosing to stay at home with their young babies. Given both the evidence of what women chose when given the choice and the risks of very early group childcare, there was a strong argument that one year of paid leave was highly desirable. But it was also very expensive. It was pointed out that paid maternity leave would not help the very poorest women, those who are not in paid work before pregnancy. The decision was taken to extend paid maternity leave to nine months in the first instance, with a commitment to a full year by the end of the parliamentary session, that is, 2010. The current government is considering adding an additional month of leave, that is nine months paid leave and four months unpaid leave. They are also very supportive of allowing shared leave between mothers and fathers.

The second aspect of flexibility was about the availability of childcare in different settings. The strategy committed the government to increasing the amount of free *childcare* from 12 and a half hours per week to 15 hours per week, again with a longer-term commitment to 20 hours per week. The 12 and a half hours came out of traditional nursery education hours, that is, half-day sessions, five days per week, in term time only. It was already the case that if parents chose to, they could use their *free nursery education hours* in settings that provided full-time day care, thereby reducing the costs of childcare. But there was no flexible offer of hours delivered from nursery education settings. If parents wanted their child to go to a nursery class in the state sector, and wanted to work 15 hours per week over three days, the nursery class would still only be offered over five days, so for some of the time a parent was at home, their child would be in nursery class, and for some of the time the parent, usually the mother, was working, the childcare would be paid for, and in a different setting from the nursery class. Many parents preferred nursery classes because they were linked to primary schools. The child was often more likely to get a place in the preferred primary school if they had already been enrolled in the attached nursery class. For the child, it meant fewer problems with transition if they attended pre-school in the school they would be attending at five years of age. The intention was to offer the flexibility of hours in any setting, that is, the statutory setting would either have to offer more flexible hours, or make arrangements for children to be moved from one setting to the next so that the parent working a full day would not have to leave work or make arrangements for the child to be picked up from nursery class and taken to a childcare setting.

This promise of flexibility was to be a big help for parents working part or full time. The tension came with the third of the big issues, 'quality'. All the evidence presented for the strategy indicated that the best quality was found in state education settings, that is, nursery schools and classes (Sylva, 2010a, p 79). While the private- and voluntary-sector day care services were excellent on flexibility, including school holidays and earlier starts and later finishes, they were less good on quality. It was very difficult to determine if the flexibility itself reduced the quality of experience for the child, or if there were other factors. It turned out that the key factor in quality was staff qualifications, particularly teachers. Nursery classes and schools had less generous staff ratios, but better-qualified staff, and worked to a more rigorous curriculum (Sylva, 2010a, p 85). There seemed to be a stronger ethos of learning in schools than in many, but not all, of the childcare settings. The strategy addressed this by committing an initial pot of £125 million each year from April 2006 to building a more qualified workforce. There was also a commitment to a new qualification for early years that would be equivalent to a graduate teacher qualification, the Early Years Professional Status (EYPS). As yet, there are not enough people who have this qualification to test out its comparability to teacher status. Experts in education are not hopeful that it will be as good. Given the very low starting point on qualifications in childcare settings, investing in staff training and increasing the proportion of qualified staff had to be sensible, but it continues to be unclear if many private and voluntary settings can match the learning ethos of schools. It was also difficult to attract teachers to the private- and voluntary-sector provision because the pay and conditions in the non-state sectors were considerably poorer than the statutory school system: longer hours, no school holidays and usually lower pay.

Can we balance flexibility and quality? The strategy was not explicit, and the big arguments came later, when designing the legislation and then the regulations. Would a child get the same benefits of attending a high-quality centre with qualified teaching staff if attending two full days a week, rather than every morning five days a week? Clearly for the employment agenda, flexibility was key, but would it serve the child development goals? Evidence was weaker in this area, but there is always common sense to rely on. In discussing this issue with Beverley Hughes, I raised a not unlikely scenario. A lone mother wants to work the afternoon shift at the supermarket. She would like her free hours spread over five days a week, three hours a day from 3 pm to 6 pm. Government policy wants this woman to work; it will reduce the risk of poverty for her and her child, and there is also good evidence that work has other benefits for adults: a lower risk of mental illness, social contact and contributions to a pension, reducing the likelihood of poverty in old age (Marmot, 2010, p 68). In terms of the life cycle, working is good for the mother and for the child. The question on quality is whether the child can gain the same benefits from attending a childcare setting from 3 pm for three hours, as she would gain from attending from 9 am for three hours. At this meeting, I was asked by an advisor if there was any research evidence that young children are less likely to learn late in the afternoon than in the morning or early afternoon. As far as I was aware at the time, there was no research evidence about the best time of day for cognitive experiences to benefit child learning outcomes.

But having worked in nurseries, I know how exhausting it is, and how it feels at the end of the day. Even if the child comes in energetic and ready for learning at 3 pm, the staff will be clearing up, the other children will be tired and most likely they will be playing outdoors or watching television. It would be prohibitively expensive to try to create a similar cognitive experience for children at the end of the day as one gets at the beginning, or even at the beginning of an afternoon session. Fortunately, Beverley Hughes agreed that completely flexible arrangements would not deliver the same longer-term outcomes for children that attending a high-quality nursery class five days a week in the morning was shown to deliver. These were very difficult debates, not least because poverty is bad for children, so anything that will reduce poverty may outweigh the benefits of limiting flexibility. Ruth Kelly, then at the Cabinet Office, and Patricia Hewitt at the DTI were both in favour of complete flexibility. Margaret Hodge, and then Beverley Hughes, both DfES ministers, wanted a balance between the indirect benefits of employment and the direct benefits to the child of a high-quality group experience. Interestingly, Ray Shostak, at the Treasury, was persuaded by the quality arguments. This is not surprising as he had come into the Treasury from the role of Chief Education Officer in a local authority, albeit one that under his leadership had pioneered much of the service integration long before 2003 that was promoted by the ECM agenda.

'Affordability' was the final of the four big issues. Obviously linked to issues of quality and flexibility, the debate was about supply-side versus demand-side funding. Do you give money to those who deliver childcare to enable them to reduce their fees, or do you give parents more money in their pockets to choose the childcare they prefer? This debate took on an ideological feel. Supply-side funding could be linked to quality requirements; demand-side funding argued that the government trusts parents to know what is best for their children. A government that was encouraging parents to choose the right school for their children, and even encouraging wider choice in health provision, could not then say that parents could not be trusted to choose the childcare that suits them. The alternate argument is that choice always favours the well informed. Furthermore, parent satisfaction with provision could not be assumed to have a direct relationship to quality of service. Indeed, research in New Zealand found that there was no relationship between research-based measures of quality and parent satisfaction (Smith and May, 2006, p 108). Parents are very reluctant to say that the childcare they use for their children is not good. Guilt is a common feature of working mothers. The childcare one uses must be good; otherwise how could you leave your child in a service that was not up to scratch? As with all other choices in public services, in my view, choice will benefit the better off. So the affordability issue was resolved with a mix of both supply-side and demand-side funding, including increases in the level of funding available to parents through the childcare element of Working Tax Credits, while supply-side issues were dealt with by the additional funding for quality.

Lots of promises

There were several other commitments in the strategy, some concerning school-aged children and Extended Schools provision, others about creating Children's Centres for all communities, not just the poorest areas. Margaret Hodge argued for fewer, but better-funded, Children's Centres with the full range of services. Charles Clarke thought that a Children's Centre in better-off areas could be a source of information and signposting. Key debates on what precisely could and could not be called a Children's Centre raged for several months, as did what the ongoing funding would be for the existing Children's Centres that had been SSLPs and Early Excellence Centres. The issue of ongoing funding for what were SSLPs became particularly heated, especially after the publication of the strategy.

It was decided that for the original 500 SSLPs, the average funding would be around £500,000 revenue per year. This was considerably less than the peak funding of around £800,000 that some of them had. However, the original plan was for each programme to be funded for 10 years, three years building up to peak funding, four years at peak and then three years to go down to zero. Many had not been in existence long enough to have reached their peak funding, so would not have to cut back. For others, the promise of permanence outweighed the concern about reductions. However, as was signalled in the 2002 CSR, all would come under the control of local authorities, who would have the discretion of distributing early years and childcare money much more flexibly. So no programme was guaranteed a fixed amount. The figures were indicative; used to work out the size of the Sure Start grant to go to each local authority depending on how many SSLPs they had in their area, as well as funding for childcare and new Children's Centres.

Another major task for the future was to reform the complex regulatory environment. The regulation and inspection arrangements for childcare and early education had already been brought together under Ofsted. We had lived in the past with a strange regulatory system that saw nursery classes and schools inspected by highly trained and well-paid Ofsted inspectors, while private- and voluntary-sector day care and sessional care was inspected by significantly lower-paid and less well-qualified staff from local social services departments. While Ofsted inspectors were responsible for all early education and childcare, there were still differences in ratio requirements and qualification levels between the state and non-state sectors. Furthermore, a complex range of services were offered in Sure Start programmes and Children's Centres that had not been part of Ofsted's inspection requirements. Could Ofsted be expected to give judgements about the quality of the employment advice, benefits advice or even parenting programmes on offer? I particularly remember an early meeting with Ofsted colleagues where we discussed the kind of services that would be offered in Children's Centres; health, parenting support, employment advice and so on. Ofsted was facing a major task of equipping its inspectors to judge the quality of the variety of activities in Children's Centres and, indeed, Extended Schools. Midwifery brought a particular blush to the Ofsted senior officials.

There was also a commitment to develop a single curriculum that would be required in any setting, including child-minding. The rationale was to ensure that children were not disadvantaged by the choices of childcare made by their parents, whether working or not. *The Early Years Foundation Stage* was developed to describe the single, play-based curriculum. As was often argued at the time, the needs of the three year old do not change depending on whether the child is in a private-sector nursery, a voluntary-sector playgroup or a nursery class. Most of these commitments would be swept up into legislation – the Childcare Act 2006. Indeed, many of the debates were replayed in developing the legislation and accompanying regulations.

Given the earlier concerns from both Number 10 and the Treasury about a lack of clear targets, milestones and a timetable for progress, *Choice for Parents, the Best Start for Children* was very explicit about what had to be achieved by when. Although meant to be a ten-year strategy, most was promised in the first five years. A selection of what was promised and within what timescale is set out in Table 7.1.

As the time of writing early in 2011, much of what was promised back in December 2004 has been achieved. Only the commitment to 12 months' paid maternity leave was lost because of the recession. While the Coalition government is engaged in significant reductions in public services, commitments to early years and childcare seem to have escaped the worst so far. However, the removal of the ring fence around funding for early years services and Sure Start Children's Centres is putting services at risk. The achievement of over 3,500 Children's

Table 7.1: Commitments in the ten-year strategy

2005	• Increase childcare element of Working Tax Credit • Consultation on maternity pay and flexible leave • Revised code of practice on nursery education • Consultation on workforce issues • Consultation on reform of regulation and inspection framework
2006	• Entitlement to 12.5 hours free early education increased from 32 to 38 weeks • £125 million for quality on-stream • Consultation on new quality framework for care and education, from birth to five
2007	• Paid maternity leave extended to 39 weeks • First cohort of children with increased entitlement from 12.5 to 15 hours per week
2008	• Children's Centres in 2,500 communities • Half of all families to have access to school-based care for 5–11 year olds • One third of secondary schools open from 8 am to 6 pm, offering extended services • New legal framework for local authorities in place • Reformed regulation and inspection system for early years and childcare in place
2010	• All parents of three- and four-year-olds offered access to wrap-around childcare linked to early education offer, available all year round from 8 am to 6 pm • All parents of children aged 5–11 have access to childcare from 8 am to 6 pm based in their school or nearby with supervised transfer arranged • Children's Centres in 3,500 communities • Goal of 12 months' paid maternity leave, with part transferable to the father

Source: HMT (2004, pp 62–3).

Centres has been remarkable. But decisions on how many centres are needed at local level and what level of funding each should get is now left to local decision-makers. The urgent will always squeeze out the important. A fragile and relatively immature system that is just taking root is clearly at risk. The final chapter of this book will go into greater detail on what has been achieved, and what needs to be done to protect those achievements through the vicissitudes of public funding regimes.

Much has been said in the last few years about what seemed to be a toxic relationship between Gordon Brown and Tony Blair. Events leading up to the launch of the strategy provide further evidence of the strained relationship. However, in the case of actual policy content, their antagonisms seemed to work to benefit children. Robert Hill, who was advising Charles Clarke at the time, and who was a key player in the negotiations between the DfES, Number 10 and the Treasury, commented as follows:

> "It was when Ed Miliband was Chief of Staff for Gordon and it was one of the periods when there was the most

productive working between Treasury, departments and Number 10.... I think Ed Miliband was a much better foil for Gordon's character and nature. They [HMT] were looking at it from a more targeted perspective whereas probably Number 10 was more looking at from a more universal perspective, and some elements were clearly about who is going to get the credit? Yes there were some disagreements, but that is only to be expected when you are making major policy. I look back on that period of policymaking in a relatively positive way. The joint working was very productive."

Carey Oppenheim also commented that, in the case of this particular policy area, the rivalry between the Chancellor and the Prime Minister had some positive results:

"If I think about the time when we were working on the Ten Year Childcare Strategy, that was absolutely when there was competition between the two of them.... So it felt that actually it raised the game, it meant that you had the two most senior people, the Prime Minister and the Chancellor, competing for being bold on childcare and children's services and Sure Start and family-friendly leave, and therefore that made us have more radical and far-reaching policies than we would have otherwise had."

As a civil servant, it cannot get much better than having both the Prime Minister and the Chancellor competing for the credit associated with your policy area.

Launching the strategy

The Ten Year Strategy was published as part of the Public Budget Report (PBR) in early December 2004. A month earlier, the Prime Minister spoke at the annual conference of the Day Care Trust, leaking some of the strategy commitments, but given the rivalry for credit, this could not be helped, and increased the interest in what the final document would say. It would be important to get the key stakeholders in early years and childcare to support the strategy, so a launch event was planned. The Chancellor would make the PBR statement in the House of Commons, and then we would release the full report. We decided to hold the event in Number 11 Downing Street, with a large closed circuit television screen set up so that invited guests could watch the Chancellor give his speech as it was happening down the road. The speech was to start at lunchtime, so I checked with the Treasury that they had organised some food for our guests. Sometime in the middle of the morning someone from Number 11 rang one of the staff in the Sure Start Unit to say they could not get the television to work. I am not quite sure what we were supposed to do, but eventually the problem was identified. They had the wrong kind of aerial. However the right aerial was in Number 10. Such was the antagonism at the time between the Prime Minister and the Chancellor that it turned out to be extremely difficult to get workmen in Number 10 to agree to move the aerial down the internal corridor that connects the two terraced houses. Carey Oppenheim solved the problem by taking the aerial through to Number 11 herself. The format for the event was to watch the speech, and then soon after have a panel question and answer session. Ed Miliband was to welcome the guests with a short speech, and then I was to chair the panel. Panel members were the Chancellor, Margaret Hodge and Phil Collins, who had done significant work on childcare while at the New Economics Foundation.

The event went extremely well. A very large number of people stared at a television screen listening to the Chancellor talk about the usual things in a PBR speech: prospects for the economy, interest rates in Japan, monetary and fiscal issues and so on. We all pretended to look interested. And then he spent a full 15 minutes describing the commitments in the Ten Year Strategy. It really was fantastic. Most of the people in the room had been campaigning on these issues for 20 years or more. For the first time, issues of childcare policy were seen as a vote-winner. As was discussed in Chapter Two, the role the Treasury was now playing in domestic policy was unprecedented, and the two most powerful men in government, the Prime Minister and Chancellor of the Exchequer, really cared about these issues.

The strategy was warmly received. Indeed, the only major complaint was the title itself. Some early education advocates were happy with the content, but disappointed that the title only referred to childcare, rather than *early learning* and childcare. This was taken on board five years later when the government published an updated strategy, *Next Steps for Early Learning and Childcare: Building on the 10-Year Strategy* (DCSF, 2009). This later document maintained all the key principles in the 2004 strategy and, as it says in the title, built on them, arguing that the next big steps were to simplify the funding arrangements and to continue to build quality.

Not everyone is happy

There was a weekend conference following the launch, mainly on early years and parenting. Many of the key players involved in the development of the strategy were attending, including Ed Miliband, Carey Oppenheim and Margaret Hodge. Also attending was Norman Glass, now Chief Executive of the National Centre for Social Research, and still taking a keen interest in Sure Start as well as wider child and family issues. I was giving a speech in Birmingham on Friday morning to Sure Start managers about the changes ahead, and then speaking on parenting at the Oxford conference in the afternoon. Margaret Hodge had to pull out at the last minute, so asked me to give her speech as well. Hence, I had a pretty full day, a major speech in the morning in Birmingham, then two speeches in the afternoon in Oxford. Disaster struck in the morning. I realised on the train up to Birmingham that I had left my papers for all three speeches on the kitchen table. Birmingham was OK; I knew what I wanted to say, but Oxford, especially giving Hodge's speech, was a real problem. Couriers could not deliver the papers to Birmingham in time, and taking them to Oxford would not give me the time on the train from Birmingham to Oxford for preparation. In the end, my husband saved the day by driving to Birmingham with the papers. All three speeches seemed to go reasonably well. The Birmingham one was the most difficult, but the Sure Start programme managers seemed reasonably pragmatic about the future. The promise of ongoing stable funding, albeit on a reduced basis, did not seem catastrophic. They were appreciative of the commitment to continuity of funding and seemed to think they could make the new arrangements work.

Later the same day, at the conference dinner, over a glass or two of wine, I discussed with Norman Glass how Sure Start was changing. Exactly a month later, the front page of the 'Society' section of *The Guardian* heralded the death of Sure Start. Glass begins the article:

> Amid all the hullabaloo about the government's 10-year childcare strategy, one quite momentous change has gone relatively unnoticed: the government's much-lauded Sure Start programme has been abolished....
>
> Ed Miliband, the Chancellor's alter ego spoke about Sure Start's capacity to transform communities. Ironically the head of the Sure Start unit was in the audience and had just spent the morning telling a regional meeting of Sure Start programme managers that their programmes were

to disappear. The irony, however, went unnoticed. (Glass, 2005, p 1)

I was in New York on the day the article was published, attending my father's funeral. Thankfully, I had switched off my phone, so did not get Margaret Hodge's phone call until a couple of days later. Glass's article generated a huge debate across Whitehall, and across the wider children's policy world, on what was now meant by Sure Start. His arguments boiled down to two key objections. The expansion to 3,500 Children's Centres would mean much less funding going to SSLPs; hence, the promise of well-funded services in the poorest areas would be diluted. His second major concern was about the loss of community control. Glass believed that once local authorities got their hands on the money, not only would they spread it more thinly, but they would not protect the kind of community governance with real decision-making power for local parents that had been the hallmark of SSLPs. Near the end of the article, in what was Glass's trademark ironic tone, he explains that in trying to solve too many problems at once, local control and generous funding were being sacrificed:

> What gave way was the autonomy of the 'local' Sure Start programmes and their 'generous' funding. The programmes are to be wound up within the next two years and folded back into local government control. No more management boards with local parents and volunteers; a severe cut in the funding per head so it can be spread over 3,500 children's centres; and no more ringfencing.
>
> But don't despair, there will be a duty on local authorities to provide integrated services – so that's all right then. We all know how local authorities love underfunded mandates. (Glass, 2005, p 3)

Needless to say, both the Treasury and the DfES were alarmed. The *Guardian* story was picked up by other media, including the BBC. And it got personal. When Glass was called by his former colleagues at the Treasury and asked where he got all this information, he named me. What for me had been a friendly dinner after an exhausting day, turned out to be an inside scoop for Glass. He did not let me or, indeed, anyone else know that the article was coming out, and, of course, he did not know that it coincided with my father's death. I am sad to say that it caused a rift in our friendship that was not healed by the time Norman Glass died in June 2009.

The Guardian gave me right of reply, which was published in an article a few weeks later, *Director Defends 'Influential' Sure Start* (Eisenstadt, 2005, p 8). My view then, as it remains now, was that while I shared some of Glass's concerns, I also knew what was not working, and what was essentially unsustainable. I considered the commitment to legislate for good early years and childcare provision a major success, but one that was inconsistent with keeping Sure Start as a separate initiative. Unless it was integrated with the offer for all children, it would result in the kind of service fragmentation it had originally been established to eliminate. Much had changed in children's services since Glass had left the Treasury. We now had the ECM agenda and, with it, legislation requiring clear accountability at local level through Directors of Children's Services and elected members as children's leads. If we were expecting those Directors to plan for the needs of all the children, from birth to 19, we could not exclude the 600–700 under-fours living in a particular few streets of the borough. The other clear flaw in the Sure Start design was the number of disadvantaged young children who did not live in the poorest areas. Even with the best reach of families, by concentrating on poor areas only, we would miss about half of poor children in England who lived mainly in very small pockets of poverty in otherwise affluent areas. Developing a new programme with generous funding is enormous fun. But unless there is a clear willingness and pathway to understand the lessons from the new initiative, and build the learning into the overall system, the benefits will be missed by a good proportion of those it was meant to serve. Establishing integrated early years services through Children's Centres in every area gave us a better chance of reaching significantly more poor children. Establishing legal obligations to deliver on the strategy would make it much more difficult for future governments to dismantle. They would need to change the law.

So, did the Ten Year Strategy signal the end of Sure Start? It did indeed signal the end of Sure Start as originally envisioned by David Blunkett, Tessa Jowell and Norman Glass. Sadly, by 2008, Children's Centre guidance from the Department for Children, Schools and Families stated that what were the *management* boards of Children's Centres would in future become *advisory boards* without the kind of power held by school governing bodies. Both this change and the move to local authority control took place when Beverley Hughes was Children's Minister. She expressed both regret and the inevitability of the process:

> "I think I did discern, and I think this was regrettable,
> as a result of that change, that the kind of dead hand of

> municipals did lay itself on Children's Centres in some parts
> of the country, not everywhere, so we saw parents disappear
> from the governing boards. I don't think there is anything
> we could have done to try and contain and sustain the spirit
> of Children's Centres; it was inevitable that it had to go to
> local authorities."

She explained that the guidance on what became advisory rather than management boards was a result of a technicality on the status of Children's Centres that made them different from the way that schools had governing bodies. It seemed to me, from the discussion, that the civil servants involved were unhelpful in finding a non-bureaucratic way out of the problem. However, more recently, in line with Big Society ideas, the Coalition Government have announced their intention to include local parents in the governance of children's centres.

In reality the process of moving to more local authority control and less parental management had been going on for some time, starting mainly with the Childcare Review in 2002. In Chapter Eight we will describe the 2005 evaluation results, and how they contributed to a tarnished image for Sure Start, at least for a few years, before more positive results emerged in 2007.

EIGHT

Did it work?

By 2005, there were significant changes to the original concept of Sure Start, so the question of whether it had worked or not was confounded by the question of what it now was. From an area-based initiative of 250 local programmes, we were now tasked with delivering the commitments in *Choice for Parents, the Best Start for Children: a Ten Year Strategy for Childcare*. No longer an area-based policy for poor children, there would now be a Sure Start Children's Centre in every community, 3,500 in all. We were handing over control from Whitehall to local authorities, and we were allowing significantly more discretion on the part of local authorities in how the funding should be allocated within their defined number of Sure Start Children's Centres. What had been a programme designed explicitly for families in poor areas, was now meant for everyone, albeit with the expectation that the most generously funded Children's Centres would be in the poorest areas, particularly the original set of what had been the Sure Start Local Programme (SSLP) areas. While the funding was to be more flexible, the service model requirements were significantly tightened up. Many of the changes to the service model were a response to the evaluation results produced by the National Evaluation of Sure Start (NESS) team. Ministers took some disappointing results very seriously and used them to reshape the programme. However, virtually all ministers involved at this point, and indeed earlier on, continued to be sceptical about the evaluation design.

Chapter Five described both the process and the controversy surrounding the procurement of the evaluation for Sure Start. This chapter will:

- review some of the challenges the original Sure Start design presented in evaluating Sure Start, by comparing Sure Start to another flagship Labour policy – the National Literacy Strategy;
- describe the design of the evaluation;
- summarise the key findings of the evaluation; and
- explain how both politicians and civil servants responded to the findings and the implications this had for Sure Start.

As mentioned in earlier chapters, clashes of strongly held beliefs are as much a feature of this part of the Sure Start story as are different views about what evidence can and cannot tell us. Within a few days of launching the Ten Year Strategy, Charles Clarke was moved from the Department for Education and Skills (DfES) to the Home Office, and was replaced as Secretary of State by Ruth Kelly. As minister at the Cabinet Office, Ruth Kelly had been somewhat involved in the Ten Year Strategy, arguing against the need for a highly defined curriculum for young children and arguing for complete flexibility for parents in their use of early years provision. Margaret Hodge consistently argued for a stronger educational component, and therefore wanted a centrally determined curriculum – what became the Early Years Foundation Stage (EYFS). After the election in May 2005, Margaret Hodge was moved from the DfES to the Department for Culture, Media and Sport and was replaced as Children's Minister by Beverley Hughes. Hughes, with a background in lecturing on social work and probation, was consistently concerned with Sure Start's ability to reach the most disadvantaged, and, like Hodge, was also very concerned with the quality of what was on offer in Children's Centres. This concern was later reinforced by results from the evaluation.

The challenges of evaluation design

As described in Chapter Five, Sure Start started out as not one intervention, but 250 different interventions, which within two years became 500 different interventions. The early emphasis on a community development approach meant that there was huge variety in SSLP design. The principle was that the Public Service Agreements (PSAs) would define the outcomes, with the inputs designed by local parents and professionals working together. This made the linking of particular Sure Start processes to particular child outcomes very difficult. The initial message, particularly from David Blunkett and Tessa Jowell, was that Sure Start was for parents and children in poor areas and should largely be built on their wishes, desires and strengths. Professional agencies would be there to support them in fulfilling their aspirations for their children. Blunkett in particular was very keen to see voluntary organisations play the lead role in establishing SSLPs.

Sure Start was about joined-up government, being user- not provider-led and based on nationally defined outcomes and locally determined inputs. The contrast with another flagship government policy – the national literacy strategy – could not be greater. It was designed and led by Sir Michael Barber when he established the

Standards and Effectiveness Unit (SEU) at what was the Department for Education and Employment (DfEE) within days of the election in 1997. Barber had been advising Blair and Blunkett on education issues before the election, and had discussed with the permanent secretary at the DfEE, Michael Bichard, what he thought was needed (Barber, 2007, pp 30–1). Given Blair's very strong and public commitment to 'education, education, education', it was not surprising that much thinking and planning had gone on before Labour came to power. But the key differences between the SEU and what became the Sure Start Unit was the SEU's clear laser-like focus on a single outcome – improving educational attainment – and the degree of central control given for the task. Virtually all children were in school and were taught by teachers who shared a common professional culture and training. What schools were meant to do was pretty well understood by politicians and the general public, so improving children's ability to read was in itself not controversial. Indeed, there are very few areas of public policy that have such a high degree of public consensus. The strategy consisted of identifying the problem of poor literacy among primary-aged children, identifying methods that worked to improve literacy levels, requiring all teachers to use these methods and then training all of them to apply the methods while keeping a very sharp eye on test results to measure progress. Accurate measurement was a hallmark of all of Barber's work for the government. Moreover, national testing had been brought in under the previous Conservative government, so data systems were already in place to test the efficacy of the strategy. What was controversial, and particularly hated by many teachers, was the idea that everyone did it, and did it in the same way in every school. They greatly resented what they saw as Whitehall interference in *their* classrooms. There was further resistance when this translated into league tables for schools, and performance management for head teachers. The key point is that Whitehall had all the necessary levers to make it happen. A publicly funded service with high levels of acceptance by the public was being radically reformed. Indeed, Barber often made the point that if public education did not improve, it would be deserted by those taxpayers who could afford private provision, who would then increasingly resent paying through their taxes for public education they did not use. The aim was not to reduce choice, but to make the public system so good that it would be the obvious choice.

The differences with Sure Start go some way to explaining the difficulty of both the evaluation and performance management of Sure Start programmes. As mentioned in Chapter Three, before 1997 there was basically no standard public service for children under four in place that could be radically reformed, and there was no public consensus on what the state should offer children and families before school age. Given that there was no early years infrastructure in place, there was also no well-trained workforce available to implement the huge increase in early years services taking place. We were starting from a very different place, not quite a blank canvas, but an immensely diverse patchwork with lots of blank spaces. The literacy strategy was controlled from one department, so there was no need for complex cross-government arrangements. The delivery of the literacy strategy was in the hands of a single profession, so there was no need for complex partnerships across agencies at local level. While it was hoped that the literacy strategy would narrow the gap in attainment, it was not aimed, as Sure Start was, particularly at poor children; it was for all children. Finally, reasonable data systems were in place at school level to measure changes in test results as the strategy bedded down. Sure Start had a very complex set of aims for children who very often were not in touch with any particular public service and sometimes were in touch with a wide range of public-, voluntary- and private-sector services. The challenges of local diversity of provision, bringing agencies together and giving parents real power in the design and delivery of Sure Start programmes meant that Sure Start represented a completely different type of policy development. Finally, the people delivering Sure Start at local level came from a very wide range of backgrounds, many of whom had not worked together before the invention of Sure Start. There was a wide variety of professions represented, as well as many staff without any formal qualifications. Given the very low pay rates, it is not surprising that high staff turnover was also a problem.

Furthermore, the evaluation of Sure Start was explicitly set up *not* to be a performance management tool. There were two reasons why this was important. First, as recommended in the feasibility study, there needed to be absolute separation between Whitehall and the evaluation to ensure that government played no part in data analysis (Bynner et al, 1999). The evaluation had to be independent. Consequently, programme managers working at local level had to be assured that any information they gave to the NESS team would not be passed to civil servants. This was a new and very innovative way of working and we were very anxious that programme managers felt enabled to share what did not work as well as what did. Performance management, especially if linked to pay and rewards, could discourage honest and accurate sharing of experience. We particularly wanted to avoid the emergence of perverse strategies sometimes employed when performance is linked to rewards. Perhaps the lesson here is that the national literacy strategy had some of the key features that academics argued were essential if Sure Start was going to be properly evaluated: a manualised intervention, a clear and measurable goal, systems in place to set baselines and, therefore, measure progress, and a profession in place whose members could be trained to deliver the intervention. While the literacy strategy was not evaluated by a randomised trial, the target group for the intervention was all primary schoolchildren, who could not choose whether or not to attend school. Reaching the intended target group was not problematic. All these factors meant that the national literacy strategy was used very effectively as a performance management tool. The government was experimenting with two very different approaches to improving outcomes for children, and both clearly had their challenges. We were to learn a lot from both.

Meeting the design challenge

Given the difficulties identified earlier and in Chapter Five, the design of the evaluation was necessarily complex. The published specification requirements for the evaluation tenders asked for designs that could tell the government: whether Sure Start works at all; why and how that which works does work; which parts work best; in what circumstances it works; and how much it costs. To answer these questions, the tender document identified a series of further questions that would need to be addressed. A selection of these questions is as follows:

- How successful is Sure Start in terms of reducing social exclusion amongst children, their families, and the communities in which they live in the short, medium and long term?
- How successful is Sure Start in improving the social, emotional, physical and cognitive development outcomes for children in the short, medium and long term?
- How well does Sure Start tackle child poverty in the short term and in the longer term, and how far it breaks the intergenerational cycle of poverty?
- How well has Sure Start brought together existing services to improve coordination and effectiveness and what effects has this had on outcomes for children and families?

- How much has Sure Start led to changes in mainstream services that has resulted in better outcomes for children and their families?
- How well has Sure Start 'added value' to existing services by reshaping them? (DfEE, 2000, p 2)

Reviewing this selection of the key questions, one is struck not only by the challenge of the evaluation, but by the breadth and complexity of what Sure Start was meant to achieve. No wonder that every minister involved with the programme was confident it would solve all social ills for this and the next generation.

To answer these questions the NESS research design included five key components:

- evaluation of the *implementation of SSLPs*: key aspects of programme design, policy, practice and style, including the quantification of inputs, what services were delivered at what cost;
- *impact evaluation*: the effect of Sure Start on children, families and communities, under what conditions did Sure Start prove most effective in enhancing child, parent and community functioning;
- *local community context analysis*: the demographics of Sure Start areas, poverty levels, employment rates, crime, health and education data;
- *cost-effectiveness*: most importantly, did any outcomes justify the outlay of resources, could the same outcomes have been achieved in a more efficient way;
- *support for local evaluations*: provision of technical support for programmes to do their own evaluations (Melhuish, 2002, pp 26–31).

The most important questions for policymakers were, first, did we ask the programmes to do the right things, that is, was the basic design of the programme right? And, second, did they do what we asked them to do, that is, was the implementation as we intended? Hence, it was critical to understand variations in implementation in order to determine what worked where to deliver improved outcomes. The design ensured an interrelationship between the components so that, for instance, the cost-effectiveness module would use data from the implementation module and the local context analysis module would inform the impact module.

The local context analysis was particularly important to understand if the Sure Start areas were significantly poorer than the rest of England and, indeed, if areas changed as a result of Sure Start. It would also be useful to compare different kinds of areas, urban and rural, north and south, and the ethnic make-up of Sure Start areas. All of these factors would provide important contextual data for the implementation study and for the impact study.

The implementation module looked at six key areas: management and coordination; access for families to Sure Start provision and services; community involvement; allocation of resources; quantity of services provided; and quality of services provided. These areas were examined in three components: a national survey of all of the first 250 programmes; an in-depth study of 26 programmes; and a series of themed evaluations on issues of particular interest (among these father involvement, special needs provision and engagement with minority ethnic communities).

The impact study was the most complicated in design. While implementation design was largely descriptive, the impact study had to be quantitative, including some form of comparison between children living in Sure Start areas and those without access to Sure Start. As mentioned in Chapter Five, this was an 'intention to treat' model, selecting at random children who may or may not be using Sure Start Services, but have access to them, and comparing them to children without access. This was seen as necessary in order to ensure fair comparison between Sure Start and non-Sure Start children. As a standard randomised control trial was ruled out by ministers from the outset, the nearest approximation was to try to match poor children in Sure Start areas with poor children in areas with similar levels of poverty and other demographic characteristics. This idea became more difficult when the decision was taken to expand the number of programmes from 250 to 500. By the time the 500 programmes had been set up, there would not be enough poor areas for comparison. The solution was to use for the first phase of the impact study children in the Sure Start areas matched with children in Sure Start areas *to be*, that is, areas that had been selected for Sure Start programmes because they had similar levels of poverty, but where programmes had not yet been established. This first phase would be a cross-sectional study of 15,000 nine-month-old and three-year-old children in the Sure Start areas compared with 3,000 children in the Sure Start areas *to be*. For the next two phases, the same children from the Sure Start areas would be followed up in a longitudinal study, and compared with matched children from the Millennium Cohort Study (MCS). Hence, for the longitudinal study, children would be compared at three, five and seven years of age. (At the time of writing, the data collection on seven-year-olds has not completed.) Data was collected on randomly selected families from the Sure Start areas and from the MCS, including data on family demographics, family relationships, parental mental and physical health, home environment, child care use, community characteristics, child health and development, service use, and labour market participation.

Given the emphasis on local governance of Sure Start programmes, it seemed to make sense to require programmes to establish their own evaluations. Hence, each programme was allowed to allocate a percentage of their budget to their own evaluation. The NESS team provided technical advice for these local studies, but SSLPs made all the decisions about what to do with their evaluation budget. Programme managers were struggling to meet the aims of delivery and they rarely had experience or expertise in commissioning evaluation. Hence, the local evaluations varied in quality and were rarely robust. They were often too limited in scope to provide good information for service reform. Taken together, they were less helpful in shedding light on the key questions that we wanted the evaluation to answer.

Summary of key results: local context analysis (Barnes et al, 2003, 2007)

The first findings from the NESS study were unsurprisingly about the local context and features of implementation. As the policy was explicitly about changing outcomes for children in disadvantaged areas, the results of the context analysis were important. We needed to know if the children living in the areas chosen were significantly worse off than their peers in England as a whole. This turned out to be the case. Jacqueline Barnes led the local context analysis team. They found that:

> Low income, unemployment and child poverty in Sure Start local programme areas were all more than double the national averages;

- Within the 20% most deprived wards in England, those wards with a Sure Start local programme had lower levels of income and employment, more child poverty , poorer educational achievement and poorer health than those wards without a Sure Start local programme;
- Almost half of the children under 4 in Sure Start local programme areas lived in households where no one was working, nearly twice as high as the proportion in England;

- Young children in Sure Start areas experience more health problems. The rate of admissions to hospital of children under 4 for gastroenteritis was double the national average, 50% higher for severe injury and 30% higher for lower respiratory infection;
- Academic achievement in primary and secondary schools serving children resident in Sure Start local programme areas was lower than the average for England;
- Sure Start local programme areas suffered more crime: burglary, criminal damage and drug offences were all significantly higher. (Barnes et al, 2003, p 1)

The NESS researchers also found considerable regional variation in both the levels and types of deprivation in SSLP areas. The highest rates of worklessness were found in the north-east, north-west and inner London. Births to lone mothers and poor health indicators were also higher in the north than in other parts of the country. Unsurprisingly, poverty rates in rural areas were less severe and access to services was more challenging. Criminal damage was also higher in rural areas (Barnes et al, 2003, pp 7–10). But the important message from the local context analysis was confirmation that the Sure Start local areas selected were indeed very disadvantaged areas, and that the disadvantages in these areas were interrelated: low income, low employment rates, poor health, high crime and so on.

The local context analysis did identify changes to local areas in the first few years of Sure Start. However, while there were significant improvements in the areas, and these were greater than for England as a whole, it was difficult to link the changes to Sure Start with any confidence. Between 2000 and 2005:

- the number of workless households with children decreased, as did the number of households in receipt of income support;
- burglary, vehicle crime and exclusions from schools all reduced, but violence against the person increased;
- unsurprisingly, there was a substantial increase in the provision of crèches; full day care provision also increased, but not as much as the increases across England as a whole;
- there were improvements in child health, with fewer emergency admissions for respiratory infections and severe injuries;
- increases in the identification of children with special educational needs were also evident, which may indicate that better general health and education screening was occurring.

Some of these can clearly be linked to Sure Start, particularly the extra crèche provision and some of the improvements of health. However, improved employment could also have been affected by the New Deal for Lone Parents. Other area-based initiatives, like Education Action Zones and the New Deal for Communities, could also have been linked to these area changes (Barnes et al, 2007, p 1).

Summary of key results: implementation (Tunstill et al, 2002)

Findings from the early implementation study were also important. These findings pointed to the likelihood that the early impacts might be disappointing. It is easy when looking at them in hindsight to realise that it would have been really helpful to dampen expectations. However, in 2002, when this early report came out, expectations for Sure Start continued to be impossibly high. Jane Tunstill led the team on implementation. Their key findings, based on a survey of 118 SSLPs, were as follows:

- there were high levels of parental involvement, including parents on the management boards, and while this involvement was usually of mothers, nearly half of programme boards had fathers as members;
- the main statutory agencies and local voluntary agencies were well represented on boards;
- joined-up working was proving harder than expected, both integration of service planning and delivery by multi-agency teams was challenging;
- there was considerable variation in spend per child, with some spending up to six times more per child than the lowest-spending programmes;
- Sure Start programmes were becoming significant employers: members of the local community and professionals were working on either full-time, part-time or a sessional basis;
- ensuring all groups were encouraged to use Sure Start services was proving very challenging;
- it was taking longer than expected for programmes to deliver the full range of services; and
- many programmes were slow in getting their local evaluations started (see Tunstill et al, 2002, pp 1, 6).

Three issues from these early findings link directly to the impact findings published in 2005. Programmes were having problems just getting services going. They were also having problems in reaching all groups who were meant to benefit from Sure Start. Finally, at this early stage, many programmes had not yet set up their local evaluations, so data collection was usually sporadic and/or inaccurate.

From the local context analysis we knew that very poor areas had been selected for SSLPs. We also knew that there were improvements in the areas over time, but these improvements could not with confidence be solely credited to Sure Start. From the first implementation study we knew that programmes were well engaged with local communities, working hard to engage families, but were finding getting services going on the ground and securing real join-up with relevant agencies hard going. One issue was becoming increasingly clear; the skill set required to run a Sure Start programme was demanding. There was a short supply of individuals with the right combination of community skills, high-level knowledge about young children and parenting, and the ability to work across different management levels and different professions. There were some brilliant local managers, but there were many others who were clearly struggling.

Summary of key results: cost-effectiveness (Meadows, 2006)

Cost-effectiveness assessments for early intervention programmes are notoriously difficult. Probably the most famous of the value-for-money investigations is the American High Scope programme, which followed children over 40 years. High Scope used a randomised control trial model for evaluation. The intervention was targeted at high-risk children, had a highly structured approach initially on one site and the original sample was only 123 children, all African-American. There were indeed huge savings over many years in costs to the taxpayer from children who had attended High Scope. However, the key savings were in the criminal justice field, that is, children who had been through this high-quality early years programme were less likely to wind up in prison. Hence, the savings became evident at least 15 years or more after the intervention (Barnett, 1996). Clearly, the cost-effectiveness of Sure Start will not really be known for some years to come in terms of the expected long-term social outcomes: less crime, better employment rates, fewer teen pregnancies and fewer benefit claimants. The first children to be born into fully functioning Sure Start areas are now only about seven years old. Moreover, the changes to the funding arrangements in 2006, when local authorities were free to distribute money more thinly across a larger number of Children's Centres, makes the allocation of funding to long-term outcomes very difficult.

Still, there are some important lessons from this module of the NESS work. The key findings from the cost-effectiveness study related to the differential spending across programmes. The most evident of these findings related to economies of scale. Small programmes were spending more per child, and a higher proportion of their funding was spent on support rather than direct service costs. By the fourth year of operation, small programmes serving fewer than 600 children were spending £1,351 per child; large programmes serving 800 or more children were spending £731 per child:

> The model of delivering services through small, freestanding local organizations working in partnership has the inevitable consequence that non-service costs (management and administration, development and evaluation) will be a relatively high proportion of total costs. Partnership working also imposes costs on other partner organizations, which are largely hidden, but are still a consequence of the existence of the Sure Start local programme. (Meadows, 2006, p 3)

Looking at spend in programmes also supported the evidence that programmes were taking much longer to get started than had been anticipated. Most programmes were not spending their full revenue allocation until their fourth year of operation. Consequently, the ratio of funding spent on service delivery as against administration also changed for the better as programmes matured. The exception to this finding was health-led programmes, which seemed to be able to get services up and running more quickly and, hence, spend more money in the first two years of operation, although their funding per child tended to be lower than most other agency-led programmes by year four. Table 8.1 shows average expenditure per child by lead agency and year of operation, comparing year one and year four.

As reported later, the health-led SSLPs also tended to have greater positive outcomes for children and families. The speed of getting started can probably be explained by the likelihood that health agencies already had a fully functioning administrative support system in place, and had much better access to data on pregnant women and new mothers. Indeed, a common complaint among programmes not led by health was the difficulty in getting health agencies to share their data.

While Sure Start programmes were successful in attracting additional resources and gifts in kind from local agencies, there was evidence that

Table 8.1: Average expenditure per child by lead agency in year one and year four

Lead agency	Spend per child in year one (£)	Spend per child in year four (£)
LA education	221	862
LA social services	168	978
LA other	169	997
Health	294	837
Voluntary or community	234	959
Other	216	821

Source: Meadows (2006, p 34).

both parents and local professionals felt discomfort at the seemingly very generous funding allocated to relatively small geographical areas, compared to what was available for older children in those areas, and what was available for younger children in areas that were often in very close proximity to the Sure Start areas. The decision to relax the clear catchment requirements was influenced by these concerns. As Sure Start matured and local people became aware and appreciative of the services, it became untenable to deny families with similar needs access simply because they lived two or three streets outside the originally determined catchment area. Indeed, it is evidence of success locally that most complaints about Sure Start were from those who wanted the service, but were just outside the catchment. Inevitably, this resulted in spreading the funding somewhat more thinly, as was predicted by Norman Glass.

My own view is that there was one other risk associated with the generous local funding of Sure Start. Many programmes secured professional staff like health visitors and speech therapists by seconding them from the NHS, and paying for them. Ironically, this worked against service integration in that Sure Start was buying services from statutory agencies, rather than encouraging agencies to contribute and work with them. While it created inter-agency teams within the SSLPs, it did little to secure the wider service collaboration that had been envisaged. It also made it more difficult to maintain these specialist services as revenue funding reduced.

Summary of key results: the first child and family impact study

There have been three major reports on the child and family impact of SSLPs (NESS, 2005, 2008, 2010). The first report received the most press attention, and led to a loss of confidence in Sure Start for some time. The second, more positive, report received significantly less attention, but was reassuring in that it confirmed that action taken as a result of the first report was having a positive impact. The third report, although positive on the adult impacts, was reporting little impact on child outcomes.

As explained earlier, the first phase of the impact study was a cross-sectional study of nine-month-old and three-year-old children and their families living in SSLP areas, and compared them with children of similar ages and characteristics living in areas that had been designated for Sure Start but had not yet received their funding, that is, Sure Start areas *to be*. The second and third impact studies were longitudinal studies of the children who were nine months old in the first impact study, and compared them to similar children taken from the MCS.

The early impact results (NESS, 2005; Belsky and Melhuish, 2007) showed that there were some small positive effects in a number of areas for the majority of families in the study. In particular, non-teen mothers, 86% of the sample, showed less negative parenting and the three-year-olds of non-teen mothers exhibited fewer behaviour problems and greater social competence than children living in the Sure Start areas-to-be. However, three-year-olds of teen mothers living in Sure Start areas scored higher on behaviour problems and lower on social competence and verbal ability than three-year-olds living in the Sure Start areas to be. Children from workless households and from lone-parent families scored lower on verbal ability than those in the Sure Start areas-to-be (NESS, 2005; Belsky and Melhuish, 2007). While limited or no impact would have been disappointing, the finding that a small number of children living in Sure Start areas were actually doing worse than their counterparts in equally poor areas was deeply depressing. The interpretation by many was that Sure Start had been hijacked by the middle classes who were shutting out the most disadvantaged. Nearly a year after the results had been published, a *Times* headline read, 'Poor Turned Off Sure Start by Middle-Class Mothers' (Bennett, 2006). The NESS results on service use revealed that middle-class use of services was very low and highly localised.

In fact, the average income of the Sure Start group as a whole was low, being below or only slightly above the poverty line. When subgroups were analysed, the teen mothers were significantly poorer than the non-teen mothers, with most teen mothers being below the poverty line. The non-teen mothers were not well heeled. We were talking about poor and very poor. However, we consistently failed to get this message across. In my view, this was largely due to a London effect. The journalists and policy commentators were often living in the areas of London where there was a mix of rich and poor populations in very small geographical areas, Hackney and Islington, for example. Hence, these same commentators, if they had small children, would have a Sure Start leaflet through their own door, the experience that upset Lord Adonis, as described in Chapter Seven. Many would have wandered into their local Sure Start and perhaps seen women that did not look quite poor enough. When asked about the takeover by middle-class parents, Yvette Cooper commented that this was the first government programme aimed at poor people that middle-class families wanted to use. Was that not a sign of success?

These first impact results, published at the end of 2005, were known to the Department for Education and Skills from June 2005. The Secretary of State, Ruth Kelly, was so concerned about the negative aspects of the results that publication was held off until further work was done to explain the results and to give a clear plan for addressing the problems they raised. However, news was leaking out. In September, the specialist publication *Nursery World* warned that there would be an onslaught of criticism of Sure Start when the impact evaluation results were published (Curnow, 2005). We were under intense pressure to publish the evaluation results. Most Labour ministers were still supportive of the programme. They often thought it was the evaluation and not the programme itself that was at fault. This was clearly Yvette Cooper's view, who, ironically, turned out to be one of the families in the study while on maternity leave. She commented when interviewed for this book:

> "I had this poor researcher come round to ask me all these questions because I came up through the random allocation in Sure Start, and I thought then that actually the evaluation was going to produce the wrong results because the questions that I was being asked didn't fit with my conception of what the purpose of Sure Start was, nor did they actually seem designed to pick up any benefits, and in our area Sure Start had only just got going and it had only been going for about six months. I'd had a couple of contacts from the Sure Start centre for Jo, but not very much and that was partly because they were still at the early stages."

Beverley Hughes was particularly frustrated that we could not know from the research whether those in the sample had actually had contact with Sure Start even though the evaluation did record service use. The sample was randomly selected from people living in the area, not from people known to be actually using the programmes. The problem, particularly at this very early stage of SSLP implementation, was what precisely could be defined as a Sure Start service. Activities were being set up in local libraries, community centres and pre-existing projects. While researchers asked about service use, it would have been hard to know if the response was about an added service as a result of Sure Start, or a better, more integrated service as a result of Sure Start.

David Blunkett, while not specifically criticising the evaluation, was still a great believer in Sure Start. He commented:

> "why, I was so disappointed as you know with the nature of the way the research came out…. People had absorbed the messages, at least temporarily, although the programmes survived because we managed to persuade some opinion formers that it was a good idea."

The particular messages that Blunkett was referring to were about the takeover by middle-class parents. Having visited the Sure Start in his constituency many times, I know that this would not have been his experience or, indeed, mine.

Most damaging of all were the comments by the Prime Minister. While most other ministers were critical of the research, Blair used the Sure Start results to renew his interest in social exclusion. In a session for public-sector professionals held at Number 10, and reported in *The Guardian*, he commented:

> When we started Sure Start – I was a bit sceptical that in the end that we could do this – there was an idea it would lift all the boats on a rising tide. It has not worked like that. Sure Start has been brilliant for those people who have in their own minds decided they want to participate. But the hard to reach families, the ones who are shut out of the system … they are not going to come to places like Sure Start. (Wintour, 2006)

The explanation for the results can be divided into three parts. First, the generous capital funding diverted energy from getting services established. The early programmes were each given around £1 million for capital development. The kind of people who were given the jobs to run Sure Start programmes were not likely to have the skills to organise a major capital project. Enormous amounts of time and energy were spent on new-builds and refurbishment, which significantly slowed the delivery of services. Second, as Yvette Cooper commented, even by the time the early data was collected on the families, many Sure Start programmes were not fully functioning. Consulting with local people on what was wanted, getting buildings built for activities to take place and working with local agencies to deliver the services were all enormously time-consuming. Third, in my view, the community development approach was also partly at fault. The most willing would be the first to come along and get involved, and these were likely to be somewhat less disadvantaged.

Programme managers were strongly encouraged and praised for engaging local parents and giving them real power in running programmes. In the poorest communities, the slightly less poor are highly likely to exclude the poorest. In the case of teen parents, very young mothers might feel patronised by the mothers only a few years older but seemingly infinitely more experienced and confident. The mothers who did come were themselves delighted with Sure Start, were very appreciative of staff and were particularly skilled at taking up time. Workers were kept very busy with women who were both very appreciative and seemed to need the services they asked for. There was a great sense of success because levels of satisfaction among users of Sure Start were exceedingly high. Ministers visiting SSLPs were introduced to women who consistently told them that the programme changed their lives, how little there had been in the community before and how much they appreciated the new services. Given this group of highly satisfied and time-consuming customers, there was little time left to make contact with those not coming. Figure 8.1 outlines the matrix I would use when talking to programme managers about the problems of reaching those not engaged.

The point of the matrix in Figure 8.1 is to emphasise the importance of knowing the local community and segmenting the market of potential users so that those who have most to benefit, but are probably the most resistant, would be encouraged to use the services. It was likely that staff were spending most of their time in the top two boxes in the early days, rather than the bottom right. In part, this explanation about the ability of SSLPs to reach the most disadvantaged families is supported by another finding that received little attention: SSLPs led by health organisations tended to have better results than those led by other statutory or voluntary agencies. As mentioned earlier, it is likely that this was a result of better access to local data on families, and possibly more highly trained staff (Belsky et al, 2007). Non-health-led programmes had difficulty finding new customers because they could

Figure 8.1: Wants and needs

Wants: yes Needs: yes *Ideal users, grateful and compliant*	Wants: yes Needs: no *Benign neglect; probably providing good voluntary effort and good for child mix*
Wants: no Needs: no *Ignore, probably using other local services, children fine*	Wants: no Needs: yes *Requires real resources to engage, probably not popular with other users*

not get the data, and the customers they already had were keeping them very busy.

While this is a reasonable explanation for the differential results, it does not explain why particularly disadvantaged groups were doing less well on a couple of measures. The only likely explanation that we have come up with is about the nature of the other services in the area. There were many anecdotal reports that community health services were withdrawing from the Sure Start areas, believing that the generous resources allocated to Sure Start meant that they could concentrate their efforts in other areas that did not have Sure Start. Hence, in a non-Sure Start area, a teen mother could be getting extra support from midwifery and health visiting that the health agencies assumed would be delivered through Sure Start in the programme areas.

Good news: summary of key results from phase two of the impact study (National Evaluation of Sure Start Team, 2008)

The first impact study was published in December 2005. The results reinforced many of the changes described in Chapter Seven, moving from 'Sure Start Local Programmes' to 'Children's Centres', a much clearer definition from Whitehall about what an SSLP would deliver and a much stronger emphasis on outreach. Indeed, the use of the term 'Children's Centres' was started after the 2002 Childcare Review was published. The move to tighter specification of services was, in part, a response to the evaluation and, in part, a response to the emphasis on childcare to enable parents to work. The time between the collection of data on children and published results can be as long as two years.

This second set of outcome results was published in 2008, so it is likely that the children studied for the 2008 results would have been experiencing programmes that were fully functional, spending their funding and providing a more coherent set of services. Hopefully, by now staff would be working harder to serve those that had not come forward when the programmes were still quite immature.

The results were greatly improved. Of 14 outcomes, seven showed a significant difference between SSLP and non–Sure Start areas:

- improved child positive social behaviour, interacting well with other children and other adults;
- improved child independence and self-regulation, better able to plan action;
- less harsh discipline from parents, less home chaos;
- improved home learning environment, more activities in the home conducive to learning like reading, singing and rhymes;
- parents making more use of local services;
- higher rates of child immunisations; and
- fewer child accidents.

The last two on accidents and immunisations cannot be attributed to Sure Start with complete confidence because there was a time lag between when the non–Sure Start children and the Sure Start children were assessed, which could explain the differences (Melhuish et al, 2008a). Most importantly, the results of this second phase showed no differences between particular subgroups. The children of teen parents, workless parents and lone parents were all showing similar improvements. It was deeply frustrating that these highly positive results did not get the press coverage of the earlier set. Even more frustrating was that press reports and commentators on Sure Start continued to use the earlier mixed results to criticise the programme, without making reference to the more recent, and considerably more positive, findings. Nonetheless, these findings gave ministers confidence that the changes that they had initiated were on the right track.

Summary of key results: the phase three impact on children and families study (National Evaluation of Sure Start Team, 2010)

Publication of the third outcome study was delayed by the impending election and did not occur until after the government had changed in 2010. While all three political parties went into the election in May

2010 supporting Sure Start, it was clear after the election that the Conservative–Liberal Democrat Coalition government would want to change the Children's Centre model considerably. Their initial comments were about returning Sure Start to their perception of its original purpose, that is, not a programme for all, but a programme that would reach the neediest families. Key questions on who *the neediest* are and, indeed, whether this was the original purpose of Sure Start will be explored in Chapter Nine. The results of the third outcome study are important and have largely gone unnoticed in the press and in the debates about the future of Sure Start.

This third study followed up over 7,000 five-year-olds and their families, the same children who had been studied when they were nine months old for the first impact study, and three years old for the second. They were matched again with children from the MCS, children of similar age and demographics, but living in areas that were not SSLP-designated areas. The effects for children were somewhat disappointing, with positive impacts on health and body mass index only. Children growing up in Sure Start areas were showing better health and were less likely to be overweight. For mothers and family functioning, the news was considerably better. Mothers in the Sure Start group had greater life satisfaction, engaged in less harsh discipline, provided a less chaotic home environment for their children and provided a more cognitively stimulating home environment. There were two negative impacts for mothers: in the Sure Start sample, they were less likely to attend school meetings and mothers experienced more depressive symptoms (National Evaluation of Sure Start Team, 2010). It is difficult to understand two apparently contradictory findings on mothers: greater life satisfaction and more depressive symptoms. But the impact size on these were both relatively small and may reflect mothers in Sure Start areas being more in contact with services and subsequently being more likely to report negative feelings. The consistent findings across the three-year and five-year data collections of better parenting in Sure Start areas is the most striking of the findings. Also, an additional positive effect within families was a reduction in workless households. Comparing the families from the MCS and Sure Start, over the three years of study, fewer of the Sure Start families remained workless compared to the MCS families. This was an important finding, given the current government's renewed efforts on child poverty.

It was clearly disappointing that the child effects within the Sure Start areas were so limited. The failure to detect improved cognitive effects from Sure Start is disappointing, but not really surprising. Cognitive impacts can largely be seen from high-quality early education, not from service integration (Sylva et al, 2010). This view was also supported by the finding that child language development was better in Sure Start areas receiving better-quality pre-school care and education (Melhuish et al, 2010). Both surprising and disappointing is the evidence on improved parenting not showing demonstrable impacts on children's social and emotional development. This could be a consequence of the need for more time being required for the effects for children to become evident. However, these results should be seen within the wider policy context and changes overall in England during the period of study. Significantly, almost all of the MCS children would have had the opportunity to attend the universal free early education offer, more than would have been the case in the earlier study of three year olds. It also needs to be remembered that, from 2004 onwards, SSLPs did not need to be so restrictive about access to services within the catchment areas, so it is possible that some of the MCS children would have been accessing Sure Start services. Hence, the Sure Start children had not fallen behind from the improvements in the earlier study; the non-Sure Start children had caught up. It is also possible that the wider changes instituted through the Every Child Matters agenda, were taking hold at local level, and appropriate support was increasingly available for disadvantaged children in non-disadvantaged areas. When Sure Start was still an area-based initiative, Charles Clarke once asked me whether we should have Sure Start everywhere. My answer to Clarke was that we should *need* it nowhere. If the policy aims of Every Child Matters were realised, then all families would get the appropriate support they needed at the right time to ensure optimal child outcomes. The intention was not to have special initiatives, but to have a comprehensive system that worked. There is one final impact study planned, likely to be published in 2012. This final study will follow the children at seven years of age.

Summary of key results: the programme variability study (Anning et al, 2007; Melhuish et al, 2007)

A further comment on the results of all three impact studies needs to be made in light of the original arguments about the design of Sure Start itself, not the design of the evaluation. Unlike the National Literacy Strategy and more like the New Deal for Communities, many different outcomes were expected of Sure Start and much was left to localities to determine. Hence, particular outcomes were likely to be unevenly distributed across programmes. Some outcomes may have been excellent in some programmes and not in others, but once combined together with overall results, there would have been significant dilution of overall effects. For example, if 10 programmes were very good at encouraging language development, and another set of 20 programmes were particularly good at encouraging healthy eating, and yet another 15 were good at getting parents into employment, there would not have been a critical mass effect on any of these outcomes large enough to register a significant impact when looking at 150 programmes. Needless to say, there would have been some programmes that were not doing well at much of anything, and others that were doing reasonably well on several measures. But teasing out the differences across programmes was essential to understand what did and did not work. Given the concern about the impact results of the first phase, a considerable amount of work was done by the NESS team in 2005 on programme variability. This study was published in 2007.

The main aim of the study was to investigate why some SSLPs were more effective in achieving outcomes than others. Basically, given the mixed results of the evaluation, we needed to know if we had asked programmes to do the right things, but they were not doing them well enough, or if the fundamental framework for Sure Start was ill-conceived. We already knew that some programmes were better than others in achieving outcomes for children. We also knew that health-led programmes appeared to be doing better. Using the guidance provided by the Department for Education and Skills (DfES) for SSLPs, a Programme Variability Rating Scale using 18 dimensions of proficiency was designed to establish more or less proficient programmes. Crucially, the researchers rating individual programmes did not have access to programme outcome results, so would not be tempted to rate highly programmes that they knew had achieved results for children. The initial results were encouraging. It was possible to identify particular aspects of programme implementation that linked to better outcomes:

- For families of nine-month-olds, more empowerment was related to higher maternal acceptance.
- For families with three-year-olds:
  - better identification of users was related to higher non-verbal ability for children;
  - better overall scores were related to higher maternal acceptance; and
  - more empowerment related to a more stimulating home environment.
- More parent-focused services were related to less negative parenting.
- More child-focused services were related to higher maternal acceptance.

- A greater proportion of health-related staff was associated with higher maternal acceptance (Anning et al, 2007; Melhuish et al, 2007).

Most importantly, programmes tended to score high, medium or low across all 18 dimensions of proficiency. High scores overall were associated with small, but significantly better than expected, child and parent outcomes. The most effective programmes were found to:

- build on the strengths of services already in place;
- put in place strong governance, management and leadership systems;
- have a welcoming, informal and professional ethos; and
- empower parents, children and practitioners.

Good programmes were particularly effective at auditing and responding to community needs, identifying and targeting children needing specialist services, recruiting and training staff with appropriate qualifications and personal attributes, and managing inter-agency team-working. However, few programmes were systematically monitoring patterns of service use, nor rigorously measuring the impact of their activities. Multi-agency working, effective information-sharing and analysis of cost-effectiveness were proving difficult for most (Anning et al, 2007).

Given that the survey was done while programmes were moving towards the more structured approach of Children's Centres, the implication of these findings was not that some SSLPs were doing well on some outcomes and others on other outcomes, as suggested earlier, but that there were not enough really good programmes to add up to overall good child and family outcomes. We had asked them to do the right thing, but we had not anticipated how challenging doing what we had asked them to do would be. Nor had we put in place effective monitoring arrangements to support those that were struggling. The question is not 'Did Sure Start work?'. The question is 'What is it about those programmes that were demonstrably delivering positive outcomes for children that set them apart from the others?'. It is critically important that the evaluation of Sure Start Children's Centres can help us to understand what the vital features are of an effective centre.

Chapter Nine will provide an overview of what we have learned from Sure Start more generally. However, the evaluation has shaken some of the core views that were held when Sure Start was set up. The findings from the Sure Start evaluation, along with the findings from the Effective Pre-school and Primary Education Project (EPPE) (Sylva et al, 2010) have been hugely influential in Britain and, indeed, internationally. Our initial belief, still held by some former Labour ministers, was that if we improved parents well-being, self-confidence and self-esteem, that in itself would lead to better outcomes for children. We have no evidence that this is the case. Absence of evidence does not mean that it is not the case; it means we cannot establish a clear link. We believed that bringing services together would improve outcomes. While it is highly likely that integrated services improve uptake, and that services that are not used are pretty unlikely to be effective, we have limited evidence that integration in itself results in better child outcomes (Siraj-Blatchford and Siraj-Blatchford, 2009). We do know that those SSLPs that were better at inter-agency working were better at producing good outcomes for children. This could also be because they tended to be better at a range of other measures of proficiency. We know from EPPE that quality matters and that quality is linked to staff qualifications (Sylva et al, 2010). Indeed, a more recent study of childcare provision done by the NESS team has reinforced the findings that quality in childcare provision can be directly linked to improved language development and, hence, school-readiness (Melhuish et al, 2010).

The argument over evaluation design will continue to run. I still believe that a randomised control trial would not have been possible with the initial programme design of Sure Start. I also believe that the evaluation was good value in that it has pointed out what we needed to do differently from the original design, that is, be more prescriptive, set up better monitoring at local level and focus services more on particular outcomes. In particular, both EPPE and NESS have taught us that if you want to change parents' behaviour, you need to be explicit about aims and choose methods that are known to work. If you want to improve child cognitive and social skills, you need to work with children and, most importantly, you need well-qualified staff with high-level skills. All these lessons have high cost implications, and Sure Start, early years and childcare are facing an uncertain future. Holding on to these key lessons will be critically important in the coming years.

Asking if Sure Start worked is clearly the wrong question. The right question is: what have we learned from Sure Start about the best ways to improve the life chances of young children? What have we learned so far that can inform policy on how Children's Centres should be configured in the future? What do we not yet know that should inform the way we evaluate Children's Centres? These questions will be explored in the final chapter of this book.

NINE

What have we learned and what have we achieved?

Chapter Eight gave a detailed summary of the results from the National Evaluation of Sure Start and other major research studies that have provided a huge amount of knowledge and understanding about what does and does not work in improving long-term outcomes for children. This chapter will look more broadly at what we have learned from Sure Start about the way government works. It will explore what ministers themselves think should have been done differently, what aspects of the programme made it particularly challenging to implement and what remains as a legacy of Sure Start. This final chapter will:

- summarise some of the key messages already rehearsed in other chapters on what we know works for children;
- describe some broader lessons about the difficulties of moving from innovation to the creation of an overall system in public services;
- give the views of ministers themselves on what they, in retrospect, think should have been done differently; and
- give some views about both the legacy of Sure Start, and where it might go in the future.

What have we learned about improving the life chances for poor children?

Sure Start was established because of a wealth of evidence that what happens to children in their earliest years has a huge impact, for good or ill, on their life chances. The rationale for investing in services for young children was that if you could ameliorate the negative impact of poverty on children, you could break the cycle of deprivation. Who your parents were and where you were born did not have to be the determining factor of your own life opportunities. Throughout this book there are numerous references to research studies and programme evaluations that support this premise. However, two more recent studies by Daniel Dorling, and Richard Wilkinson and Kate Pickett challenge it. They argue that ameliorating the impact of poverty will not break the cycle of deprivation (Dorling, 2010; Wilkinson and Pickett, 2010). Both these academics argue that it is inequality itself that results in poor outcomes, not poor outcomes determining life chances. Dorling, and Wilkinson and Pickett argue that the root cause of poor outcomes is not poverty per se, but the difference in incomes between the most well-off and the least well-off. They argue that countries that are more equal, that is, have a narrower span between the best-off and the worst-off, deliver better outcomes for all citizens across the income distribution. This would suggest that social mobility is impeded by the steepness of the climb. The wider the income distribution gap between the richest and the poorest, the steeper the steps are from one income quintile to the next. This not only makes the climb for those on the lower rungs very challenging, it means that those on the upper rungs will do everything they can to prevent their own children going down a rung or two. The unpalatable part of relative social mobility is that for some to go up, others must go down.

What does this mean for all our efforts to improve social mobility by improving educational and social outcomes, and, particularly for Sure Start, for improving school-readiness. First, I would argue that improving the lot of the poor is a social good in its own right, even if social mobility does not shift. Ensuring a good start in life by the provision of high-quality support for parents and high-quality early years education will provide a child from a poor background with higher-level social and cognitive skills than their peers in the same social grouping who have not had these services. As an adult, that child will be more likely to be employed and less likely to be on benefits. High-quality early education will enhance both social and cognitive skills, as will high-quality parenting. James Heckman argues that a broader range of skills than just cognitive ability are wanted by employers, among these: teamwork, concentration, reliability and persistence (Carneiro and Heckman, 2003, p 86). While improved educational and social outcomes will not in themselves make a perfect society, they do contribute to improving life chances for poor children. Waldfogel supports this view, arguing that while inequality was not shifted during the Blair/Brown years, absolute poverty was substantially reduced in families with children and relative poverty was somewhat reduced (Waldfogel, 2010). We have concentrated on shifting the curve by lifting up those at the bottom, while those at the top have increased their wealth at a faster rate. Inequality increased, but the living standards of the bottom 20% were improved (Sefton et al, 2009, p 25). The reduction in overall income inequality across all classes suggested by Wilkinson and Pickett, and Dorling is clearly desirable. But the social and economic changes required to achieve greater income equality are unlikely to be put in place over the next few years. The current challenge is holding on to the progress we have made and continuing to develop and improve what we offer to children and families, a challenge deserving of and requiring our best efforts. We can continue to improve services for young children if we learn from the experience of the last 12 years.

What have we learned about what we should offer children and families?

What has Sure Start told us about how to run early years services that impact on children's social and cognitive outcomes? The most important lesson actually comes from the Effective Pre-school and Primary Education (EPPE) studies. The most salient factor in determining positive outcomes for children is the home learning environment (HLE) (Melhuish, 2010). What parents do with children before they are old enough for school, and, as they get older, what they do with them in the hours they are not in school, has a much stronger effect on child outcomes than group care. This intuitively makes sense, in that a high-quality HLE is likely to be a constant in a child's life from birth. The key period for language development is in the first three years, when the HLE would be particularly important. The Sure Start impact studies showed better HLEs for Sure Start children than for non-Sure Start children in both the 2008 and 2010 reports. However, neither report showed differences in cognitive development, and they also showed only small improvements in social development. Perhaps, as Heckman argues, these investments very early in life take some years to bear fruit. Improvements in parenting, if sustained throughout the school years, could have a much longer-term positive impact. Most of the US studies did not begin to show real returns until children were of school-leaving age. I am optimistic that this will be the case. Meanwhile, the current emphasis on embedding more structured evidence-based programmes into Sure Start Children's Centres should result in greater impact. There are some parenting interventions that already have a very strong evidence base for improvements in behaviour and family relationships. Less evidence is available relating to programmes that work with parents of children under three, the key period for language development. The Nurse Family Partnerships programme is a notable exception. It has a strong evidence base of success and is aimed particularly at young mothers and fathers, working intensively with families during pregnancy and the first 24 months (Olds et al, 2004). Incorporating the use of such interventions into good practice in Children's Centres is essential, and is a high priority in the model of Children's Centres emerging from current government policy. It is also vital that we provide both informal community-led and more structured intensive support for particular groups in the very earliest months of life.

EPPE demonstrated that quality in early education and childcare improves cognitive and social outcomes. However, the impact size, that is, how much difference quality makes, is smaller than the difference the HLE makes (Melhuish et al, 2008b; Sammons, 2010). Delivering high-quality group care requires well-qualified staff with strong leadership and an in-depth understanding of child development. With appropriate resources, this can be done. The overarching message is that quality early education does make a difference and can be done; improving how parents interact with their children at home makes a bigger difference, but is harder to do. By concentrating effort on quality in early years settings, we can make a small impact on a very large number of children. The potential impact of improving the HLE is much greater, but it is much more difficult to achieve. This makes a strong argument for the importance of maintaining what is now the universal offer of 15 hours per week of early education for all three and four year olds, *and* developing more intensive, targeted programmes for children under three – a renewed and improved Sure Start.

User satisfaction: essential, but not sufficient

The overarching message from Sure Start is that the emphasis on working with adults does not necessarily deliver better outcomes for children. This is particularly true if the work with adults is not explicitly about their children. Activities designed to raise self-esteem, build confidence or generally help people feel better about their circumstances have not been shown to improve outcomes for children. To improve outcomes for lots of children, universal high-quality early education is the key. To improve outcomes for particularly disadvantaged children, work with parents needs to be focused on the needs of their children, delivered with clear aims and designed to ensure progress can be measured. The myriad of activities that many Sure Start programmes organised for parents were sometimes not sufficiently focused on child objectives. There was a belief among some programme managers and, indeed, some ministers that parent satisfaction was the key to improving outcomes. Our hardest lesson has been that parent satisfaction is only part of the story. Mothers and fathers liking what is on offer in a Sure Start Local Programme

(SSLP) or Children's Centre is *essential* to ensure engagement, but it is not *sufficient* to ensure improved outcomes for children. The key to success is informal activities to ensure participation of the widest possible group and specific, well-tested targeted interventions with parents to improve child outcomes. To date, Sure Start has been more successful in improving outcomes for parents, which it is expected will eventually improve outcomes for their children. Some significant adult outcomes have been demonstrated, particularly the reduction in worklessness among the Sure Start families. Given the correlation between long-term worklessness and poor outcomes for children, this is an important success indicator. However, for particularly poor children, a combination of quality interventions with mothers and fathers around birth and for the first three years, combined with high-quality early education and encouragement towards employment, all need to be in place to have the maximum impact. The best Sure Start Children's Centres are delivering such a package, but it is by no means in place everywhere, or even in the poorest areas. The concerted effort must now be to build the skills of engagement and the skills of local managers in selecting appropriate evidence-based interventions while maintaining the informal and welcoming ethos that has made Sure Start Children's Centres so enormously popular with families. The building of the quality of leadership and management in Children's Centres will, in the medium to long term, improve outcomes for children.

Finally, we have learned that to ensure reach to the neediest, a universal platform is essential. About half of poor families do not live in poor areas, and there will be a small number of families who are not poor but have complex problems and need support. Furthermore, families move in to and out of difficulty and the right level of light-touch support at crucial times can prevent decline. This is early intervention not with a specific programme, but with a sensitive and well-trained member of staff who can spot difficulties and offer help well before things deteriorate. A universal platform of Children's Centres makes this support for families on the cusp of difficulty much more likely.

Was it simply too hard?

As was described in Chapter Three, the design of Sure Start was in part based on submissions from practitioners in the field and stakeholders from a wide variety of organisations who had been running community-based programmes for a number of years. Actual evidence that any of these programmes delivered outcomes for children was thin, largely because in Britain there had been little rigorous evaluation. So the programmes that had been identified as proving that early intervention could work were mainly US programmes that bore little resemblance to the original design of Sure Start. Moreover, the stakeholders who held great sway over the officials designing the programme were extremely convincing. They promoted approaches that were consistent with the vision that both David Blunkett and Tessa Jowell had for Sure Start. They were highly articulate and successful campaigners for early years programmes. But they were not representative of the early years workforce. They were extraordinary individuals who had been running innovative programmes for years. What I now believe we failed to understand at the time is how difficult the task of running a Sure Start programme would be. Bringing together local providers in different agencies, developing programme plans with local parents, commissioning major capital projects and an in-depth understanding of early childhood development were all essential skills and activities for SSLP managers. There were extraordinary people who were active in advising on the design of Sure Start. Among these were Gillian Pugh, who was then running Coram Family, Bernadette Duffy, head of early education at Coram Family, and Margie Whalley, who had established Penn Green, perhaps the most internationally well-known Children's Centre. These individuals were the exception, not the rule, and they could not be cloned. Norman Glass believed that their energy, enthusiasm and creativity would be replicated across the country if we freed up local areas to design their own programmes, albeit with a clear set of outcome requirements set out in the Public Service Agreement (PSA). I believe a major failure was to underestimate the skill set required to deliver a high-quality Sure Start programme.

Organisational theory provides another way of looking at this problem. Henry Mintzberg describes how work is structured in different kinds of organisations and professions (Mintzberg and Quinn, 1996, p 335). He explains that different organisations require different levels of skill in their employees, and depending on the nature of the task and skills required, the work is either highly specified or employees have a high degree of latitude in carrying out their responsibilities. Employment with low qualification entry barriers tends to be highly structured, with clear protocols and systems for how tasks should be carried out. These jobs tend to pay low wages and have very clear hierarchies and lines of accountability. Employment with very high qualification entry barriers tend to pay more, have weaker hierarchies and have considerable freedom of action once one is admitted to the profession. Hospital consultants are notoriously difficult to manage as their managers are, in their eyes, less well qualified than they are. Academics are promoted usually through peer review, not through university hierarchies. Moreover, surgeons are not resistant to following specific protocols set out in performing operations. They are comfortable with evidence-based practice precisely because they understand the science behind it and because it was designed by their peers, not their managers.

Returning to Sure Start, early years staff with university degrees were pretty thin on the ground, and entry requirements were low for the vast majority of workers in childcare settings. Not only were wages low for childcare workers, there was also no clear professional ladder to climb. Within education, teachers of the youngest children had the lowest status. Outside of education, there was no clear professional route for the kind of individual needed to manage or, indeed, be part of the team to run a Sure Start programme. This is not to say that there were not some outstanding Sure Start programme managers. NESS shows us that some programmes did extremely well, and the programmes that were well managed did prove more successful in improving outcomes for children. It was not only a difficult task, however, it was also a relatively new way of working. Professional groups tend to be very hierarchical. Few of the colleagues in other agencies that programme managers needed to join up with would have seen anyone working in early years as a peer, making inter-agency working particularly difficult. This argument leads to one conclusion and two implications. The conclusion, as already discussed earlier, is that we vastly underestimated the difficulty of the task. Given that, and using the Mintzberg model, we either should have made the task less challenging by more specification of how to do it, or thought more about the kind of support and training new programme managers would need. In fact, we should have done both.

In more recent years, we have made some progress on both these issues. The development of the Early Years Foundation Stage clearly gives specification on what should be done with young children in childcare and early education settings, and there has been more detailed guidance from government on what Children's Centres should offer to families. There has also been progress on improved training opportunities. The Early Years Professional Status (EYPS) allows further training for early years workers and is intended to be equivalent to graduate teacher level for staff. It is a move in the right direction, but there are as yet not enough people who have attained the qualification in practice to know if they make the kind of difference that trained teachers make when they are working in early years settings. Furthermore, there are still big differentials in pay and conditions between teachers and those with the EYPS (Taggart, 2010). Moreover, the EYPS training does not provide the kind of skill base and knowledge that would have helped Sure Start managers lead multi-agency work in Children's Centres. The challenge of managing Children's Centres has been addressed by the development of the National Professional Qualification in Integrated Centre Leadership (NPQICL). This qualification was designed specifically for Children's Centre leaders, and is delivered under the auspices of the National College for Leadership of Schools and Children's Services. However, unlike head teachers, there is no requirement to attain this qualification either before becoming a Children's Centre leader or, indeed, while doing the job. Overall, compared to the investment in teachers and teacher education, there has been limited investment in developing the early years workforce. Given the historically low base of qualifications in this workforce, we have made progress but not yet established a professional culture like that of teachers, social workers or doctors. In summary, we started Sure Start with very ambitious goals, but failed to put in either the training requirements for staff typified by professions with high entry barriers, or the work specifications typified by employment with low entry barriers, to ensure delivery of a new and complex way of working. Much progress has been made on both of these fronts in more recent years, but the low wages and, indeed, low status of working with very young children is largely unchanged.

Innovative pilot or establishing a new national system?

Sure Start started out very explicitly as an innovation. While ministers rejected a randomised control trial evaluation, they did agree to a significant sum on evaluation, and clearly wanted to know if Sure Start *worked*. As described in Chapter Eight, this was too simplistic a question. Such a complex programme would not be entirely successful or, indeed, unsuccessful. It would work in parts, and we needed to understand precisely what did work. In my view, the key problem was that, for a while, ministers could not conceive of the possibility that it would not work. This enthusiasm meant that the programme was expanded very quickly before any evidence was available. Ironically, the speed of expansion also meant that the attention that should have been given to supporting existing programmes was diverted into getting as many programmes, and then as many Children's Centres, established as quickly as possible. One critical lesson about the complexity of the task was that it took a long time to get programmes established. The requirement for local consultation, understanding what was already available for young children and putting together partnerships with the appropriate agencies all took time. There was an understandable impatience among ministers to get things going. However, in retrospect, it is clear that we were not testing a new *intervention*. We were, in Margaret Hodge's words, *delivering a new frontier of the welfare state*. Schools had been in place as an expectation of what the state offers all children for many decades. We had no such public consensus or shared expectation of what the state should offer young children. Most, but not all, of the ministers interviewed for this book felt the rapid expansion was the right thing to do. Politicians worry that they will not get a second chance to make a difference. The key task for them was to get things going, and then to change and improve as we went along, and this was pretty much how it happened. Indeed, ministers are to be congratulated for their willingness to listen to the evidence and change according to it. We may have avoided some mistakes had we taken more time, but I believe now that the ministers were right to push for rapid growth. It is likely that without the rapid expansion, there would not be the current critical mass of Children's Centres that are so popular within communities. Dismantling even a small percentage of them, as is currently likely to happen, makes front page news. The establishment of a national network of 3,500 Children's Centres in little over 10 years is a remarkable achievement. The fact that these centres are used by poor and not poor alike is to be welcomed. This surely must be the first public service designed for poor people that has been criticised because too many middle-income people like it.

There are also differing views of whether it was right to give the responsibility for Sure Start Children's Centres to local authorities. I thought that this was the right thing to do. At the time, the Every Child Matters agenda was beginning to take hold at local level. A key feature of the new way of working in children's services was the creation of the new role of Director of Children's Services. These posts ensured that there was a single person who would be held accountable for child outcomes for all children in the local area. It became untenable to keep the young children living in the Sure Start areas outside of these arrangements. We had started in 1999 with a key aim of joining up services for young children. We could not argue five years later that everything but Sure Start should be joined up at local level. Geoff Mulgan, a senior advisor in Number 10 from the start of the Blair government, holds a different view:

> "The lesson is ... this sort of new model can only grow if
> it has a fair amount of insulation and buffering from the
> rest of the system, and I guess my main critique of what

the departments did with all these programmes is that they integrated too quickly, whereas the slightly perhaps over-subtle theory of joined-up government was that you had to allow some of these models to grow in a self-contained semi-non-joined-up way and only once they had established a degree of confidence and capacity and culture would you then integrate them back into mainstream hierarchies."

Mulgan argues that real innovation takes time to settle and needs a certain degree of separateness from the mainstream before it is possible to influence the mainstream in new ways of working. Both David Blunkett and Norman Glass were also of the view that local government should not run Sure Start. However, their objections were not about the timing of innovation, but about a fundamental mistrust of local authorities to be able to run Sure Start as they intended. Their view was that local authorities would remove much of the community engagement features that were so central to the original design. Indeed, this did turn out to be largely true, but mainly because of the disappointing evaluation results which seemed to show that the local community model was not delivering results for the most disadvantaged children, those most likely to be left out in classic community development methods.

Ironically, the current government is very keen that local authorities hand over control of their Children's Centres to voluntary-sector organisations or local community organisations and they are very keen that Children's Centres reach the most disadvantaged children. Yet there is no evidence that these types of organisations are better at doing the job required. Within new thinking on Children's Centres there is an attempt to bring together two concepts that could have inherent tensions. The government is keen on payment by results and keen on increasing community participation in local services. The combining of payment by results, that is, funding based on outcomes rather than inputs, and Big Society ideas like the use of more volunteer effort and much more local community control of services could be in tension or, more optimistically, could result in new forms of organisation that solve some of these problems.

In summary, three features of Sure Start have been highly controversial: the original design allowing very high levels of community control and therefore diversity of delivery; the very rapid expansion: and the handover of control to local authorities. Hence, what started as a relatively large pilot, grew very quickly into an offer for all young children and families. Community control was championed by Blunkett, who believed and still believes that better outcomes for children will result from building social capital in communities. The rapid expansion happened in two phases; moving from 250 to 500 SSLPs was decided in 2000 because ministers did not consider the possibility that Sure Start would not work, and therefore saw no need to wait for evaluation results. The second rapid expansion announced in the 2004 Ten Year Childcare Strategy, from 500 local programmes to 3,500 Children's Centres, signalled ministers' decision to move from a targeted pilot to an overall system of provision for early years, from an area-based anti-poverty programme to a basic level of service for all young children, albeit delivered more intensively in poor areas. As Beverley Hughes explains, the establishment of a national system meant that the move to local authority control was inevitable. Ministers want new policies and are impatient once an announcement is made to get on to the next project. A slower, more measured approach would probably have resulted in a higher-quality programme, with incremental learning. But it would have been a better service for significantly fewer children. It would not have had the profile, both good and bad, that Sure Start has had, and would have been much more vulnerable to the cuts announced by the Coalition government in the autumn of 2010.

What do ministers think now?

All the ministers interviewed for this book were asked what they thought should have been done differently, and what they are particularly proud of. The following outlines a selection of former ministers' retrospective views of Sure Start.

As mentioned earlier, David Blunkett is still of the view that Sure Start became over-professionalised and that the control of local government weakened his vision of what Sure Start should be:

> "I don't think it could have worked without local government's benevolent support but that is a different matter to incorporation. This is the way local government is generally. If you talk to local community bodies that are trying to develop an alternative way of working, they find that local government offices are deeply incorporating and defensive about their position, so things aren't all right unless you are part of us, and that is where I do share a view with the present government that we've got to have a much more communitarian approach ... where local government act as

the support for devolved activity within the neighbourhood, not solely as the provider."

Tessa Jowell also believes that Sure Start strayed too far from the original vision. Like Blunkett, she believes the community emphasis was right, but she also thinks the identity got confused because we were trying to do too many different things:

> "But I think where we failed was to try to shape it, to make Sure Start do too many things ... had we said Sure Start is a nurture programme for babies and infants, from 0 to 3, the purpose is absolutely clear, and then later on you have early years and childcare and mums to work....
>
> I think the neighbourhood template for Sure Start was absolutely right, which recognised that any new mum and her baby benefit from the kind of support that Sure Start can provide, and indeed mums, middle-class mums lacking in confidence get something from working-class mums who already have five children, you know there's all that.... It was always a neighbourhood programme that would bring together mothers and babies from vastly different backgrounds and I am proud of that."

Like Blunkett, Jowell thinks we should have kept Sure Start separate from childcare and early education policies, but she puts a much stronger emphasis on babies than does Blunkett. They both take a very strong community development approach and Jowell rejects the criticism of missing the poorest by stressing the benefits of the social class mix.

Estelle Morris, who followed Blunkett as Secretary of State, thinks we should have been more prescriptive. She has sympathy for the Blunkett view, but believes that community capacity did not exist to translate local design and delivery into better outcomes for children. Morris says:

> "I think it was right to say to each local community, 'How best can you deliver this?' But perhaps what we should have done was to offer six models, choose from these what will work locally.
>
> What we did with Excellence in Cities ... we said, 'We want to devolve power to you, but these six areas are the ones where we want you to achieve. Now work out how you want to do it and bring it back to us.'

I think we tremendously empowered them, the local Sure Starts, to respond to the challenge in the way they see fit, but you can't empower people unless you give them the skills to use that power, and looking back ... we just had to give them more information so that they could make wise decisions."

Morris argues that we either should have given a set of operational models to choose from, or been much clearer about outcomes. In fact, we were clear about outcomes with the PSA, but, unlike Excellence in Cities, we did not have data systems in place to measure results, nor a trained workforce to make the informed judgements on delivery required to achieve the outcomes. Morris is backing up the view that we underestimated the challenge and therefore failed to provide the level of support and guidance needed.

Margaret Hodge also has views on what could have been done differently. She is still strongly of the view that the joint ownership with health was not workable. Unlike Jowell and Blunkett, she believes the integration with the rest of the early years and childcare agenda should have been done much earlier. She also thinks that the expansion to a universal service was attempted too early:

"I think we shouldn't have tried to expand so fast. I think we tried to do too many things on not enough money because we wanted to provide a universal service that was non-stigmatised and that was always a dilemma that if you kept it as an offer in deprived areas, it would become a stigmatised service ... so there was a bit of me that wanted it universal, but also that wanted to ensure most money went to poor areas."

Hodge also differs from Blunkett's view about local government:

"Mistake number two, we should have attached it to a public service, we should not have played around with this privatisation.

So what did we get wrong? We did too many, we didn't link it into a public service, we didn't spend enough money and time on the qualifications of people working there, and it's only quality that really changes children's lives. So we tried to do it on the cheap, and we didn't get health in there."

Beverley Hughes expressed sympathy with the empowerment of local parents, but she also raised concerns about the delivery of high standards everywhere. Like Hodge, Hughes is particularly concerned with both reaching those most in need and the delivery of a high-quality service:

> "What taxed me was how you reproduced the best everywhere, that is the real challenge of anything like this, how you reproduce the best everywhere. So to some people the variation in different centres was a positive thing and it was, if it was relating to the community, but when variation actually meant things were being done to very different standards and you could see some places were really, really making a difference, and others there was a sloppiness about the approach, there was a lack of rigour, there was a lack of thinking in terms of what we were doing, and you could feel that when you walked in to centres."

As mentioned in Chapter Seven, Hughes also expresses some concern over the loss of community control. But she also expressed concern that at least some local authorities were not delivering the consistent quality that was the justification for giving them the control of Sure Start. When asked specifically about the movement of control to local authorities from Whitehall, she said:

> "In terms of the number of centres that was inevitable, they just had to, there was no way you could reach out to 3,500 centres, and I suppose what needed to happen was that the advisers in local authorities, the people responsible for the development of early years particularly, that they had sufficient knowledge and consistency amongst each other to take the programme forward."

Both Yvette Cooper and Beverley Hughes think that the variety of views ministers held about Sure Start strengthened the programme. For Cooper, it demonstrated that different bits of government could work together for a common aim of better outcomes for children, and, for Hughes, it reflected a willingness to consider the learning from the programme as we went along. Cooper remarked:

> "Whilst everybody came to it with a slightly different interest, or a slightly different angle, actually what worked was having so many people with so many different

perspectives, because if your core objective is to improve children's life chances, you won't do that just by tackling smoking in pregnancy, you won't do that just by providing extra childcare, you will only do it by addressing all of those different elements."

Hughes similarly thinks that the changes brought to the programme by different ministers should be seen positively:

"I don't see any of the slightly different phases that we went through as something we shouldn't have done in a way because the whole requirement was necessarily iterative; you could not just plan this from day one and implement it. We had to develop capacity, we had to learn from experience in different areas, and so whilst I think the shifts that I wanted to see were necessary in my view, I don't feel that the starting point was wrong or should have been done differently. I think we built on each stage."

All the ministers interviewed expressed enormous pride at having been involved in Sure Start, and many still consider it one of the major achievements of the Blair/Brown years. All talked very warmly about visits to Sure Start programmes and Children's Centres, and about the views of their constituents about the programme. Two key achievements stand out in most of the interviews: first, there is now widespread consensus that experiences in the first four years of life are critical to lifetime success or failure. Very few politicians would now express the view, which was widely held before 1997, that what happens to young children before they enter school is the sole interest of their mothers and fathers and the government should not interfere. There continues to be debate on the nature of the role of government in the early years, as in virtually every other aspect of social policy, but an ongoing commitment to quality of early years experience is evident in current UK government policy.

Second, an infrastructure is in place that is difficult to dismantle. Hodge, Hughes, Cooper and Ashton all agreed on the importance of establishing a core set of universal services that the public now expect. Hodge and Hughes particularly expressed concern about quality, and that perhaps the speed of establishing the services meant that not enough effort was expended on quality. Nevertheless, the existence of a service that can now be continually improved, as we expect with schools and health services, is a significant achievement. The National

Health Service has been around since 1948, universal state education for considerably longer. We do not ask for the *evidence base* for schools or hospitals. We ask how to improve the outcomes they deliver for the public. Usually, we improve them by using evidence-based programmes embedded in an overall system of delivery of public service. Both health and education are continually being changed in attempts to improve quality, but no one would argue about whether they *work* or not. They are part of public service systems that citizens expect from the state. In little over 10 years, we have established a basic infrastructure of universal early education for three and four year olds, greatly expanded and raised the quality of childcare and established a network of Children's Centres offering a range of services for parents and children.

Lessons for the future

The current government has expressed support for early years services and has re-energised thinking around early intervention with very young children. At the time of writing (winter 2010–11), there are at least four reviews commissioned by the government that could have significant impact on early years services: Professor Eileen Munro has published two reports so far on child protection (Munro, 2010, 2011); Graham Allen MP has published the first phase of his review on early intervention (Allen, 2011); Frank Field MP has published a report on child poverty (Field, 2010); and Dame Clare Tickell, the Chief Executive of Action for Children, is chairing a review of the EYFS. This attention and energy on children can only be a good thing for the future of children's services in England. Both the Allen and Field reviews have emphasised the importance of parenting in breaking the cycle of deprivation and improving social mobility, particularly in the first few years of life. In Munro's second report, she endorses the importance of community family support as a platform to ensure early identification of problems. All of the published reviews make valid and useful recommendations about the need for better parenting support and, particularly for Graham Allen, the importance of using evidence-based interventions that have been shown to improve outcomes. The Tickell review is likely to recommend simplifying the EYFS, which, again, is probably needed. However, we are a very long way from delivering the level of quality in early years settings that really makes an impact on school readiness. The EYFS and, particularly, the Foundation Stage Profile, which assesses school readiness for every child, are important tools in building our knowledge base about whether or not we are making a difference. Clearly these reports make an important contribution to what needs to be done to improve life chances and narrow the gap in outcomes between the poorest children and the rest. However, they are but part of a range of important lessons about systems that we ignore at our peril. They are part of a broader set of issues that need to be considered for real progress. Briefly, those lessons are about:

1. the need for reliable data – local population data to ensure engagement and child well-being measures to evaluate progress;
2. clarity and honesty on policy and practice intent – outcomes for children, for adults or for improved parenting; for reducing poverty now, or for reducing the likelihood that the current generation of children will end up in poverty;
3. the limitations and benefits of community development methods;
4. the challenges of working across agencies and across government;
5. the critical importance of staff development and improved salary and career structures;
6. the need for a performance management system that does not stifle innovation; and
7. the iterative nature of policy development.

The need for reliable data

First, we need local providers to have reliable information about young families in the area. As described in Chapter Eight, the SSLPs that had good links with health had better reach than those programmes in areas where local data-sharing was problematic. Knowing who to engage with is critical. Knowing if engagement has made a difference is also critical. Hence, we need standard measures and data sets on child well-being. If we want to improve life chances, we need to measure as we go along. Britain has led the world in longitudinal studies and, indeed, such studies have been very influential in policy development. However, the lessons learned from them are too late for the children who are long grown up by the time the patterns indicating the risks and protective factors of early experience emerge. We need some simple, real-time, non-intrusive and not terribly expensive ways of knowing what the needs of children are locally and whether we are making progress. Finding the right set of measures that deliver the kind of data that will inform practice without being overly bureaucratic is a significant challenge. This is particularly important as we devolve power to local authorities. Standard measures to establish baselines from which we can judge the success or failure of local policies are critical.

Clarity and honesty on policy and practice intent

We need to be honest and clear about policy intent. Anti-poverty strategies that concentrate on employment can indeed reduce child poverty, but if the childcare is of poor quality, it will not improve child outcomes, and if really poor, may, indeed, do damage. The debates on what age childcare is risky for children will run and run. However, there is no debate about the importance of quality at any age. The efforts to improve the experiences of children in group care need to be intensified. Quality for babies is particularly difficult, and given that we now have nine months' paid maternity leave, reducing the number of babies under one experiencing group childcare, particularly for long hours, would be a very good thing.

Conflicting intent occurs in practice as well as policy. We need to be much more rigorous in the way we work with adults, both mothers and fathers, in Children's Centres. Certain activities are effective in developing engagement, but may not have any impact on child outcomes. Mothers and fathers who are not engaged are not likely to benefit from the centre, but engagement on its own does not deliver benefits for children. Children's Centre leaders and staff should be very explicit about why they are running a particular activity and what they expect will improve as a result, and have some way of measuring whether what they hoped would happen actually occurs. This, again, returns to the earlier point on data: who are you reaching? And, as importantly, who is not coming and why? What are you achieving beyond contact that will improve the life chances of children?

Once they are engaged, what happens? Is the activity about encouraging employment through skills development, or about improving parenting skills? Both of these are very important, and some interventions can do both. Adult literacy is a good example; again, if effectively delivered, family learning programmes can improve outcomes for both adults and children. Learning to read improves employability, but also improves the likelihood that a parent will encourage their own child to read. There are a range of evidence-based programmes that have been shown to improve child behaviour through improved parenting practices. Centre staff should be trained to deliver with fidelity interventions that have a strong basis in evidence, that is, they are known to work. New interventions need to be subject to rigorous evaluation. Again, we need to develop some evaluation strategies that may not be as stringent as randomised control trials, but tell us significantly more than whether participants *liked* the programmes and providers *thought* they worked.

The limitations and benefits of community development methods

Some of the learning from Sure Start has been quite painful. Our hopes that community development methods would improve life chances for children have not yet borne fruit. There are two key points in this lesson: first, community engagement needs to be linked to who is not coming as well as who does; and, second, engagement has to be linked with clear negotiation on what users say they want and what professionals think their children need. My overall conclusion is that community development can be really positive for those who do engage, but can result in even further isolation for those who do not. The emphasis on empowering local parents, mainly mothers in the early days of Sure Start, was enormously satisfying for many mothers, but sometimes not really very welcoming for teen mothers or, indeed, fathers. Again, data is crucial. The ability to use local data to keep track of who is not coming, and having the courage to challenge those who do come to be more welcoming to newcomers, are both essential. Furthermore, as Estelle Morris commented, some communities and individuals may have limited aspirations for their children. It is the job of good early years services not only to respect the strengths of the local community, but to challenge attitudes that restrict opportunities for children. Our role is not to restrict knowledge about what is good for children for the fear of imparting *middle-class values*. The real challenge is to share knowledge in ways that build confidence in both parents and children in what is possible for the future. Using evidence-based interventions delivered by highly skilled staff is part of this picture. It is also about an ethos and atmosphere in centres that encourages learning and development for staff, mothers, fathers, carers and children. We learned that while community development methods create a fantastic atmosphere and enjoyment in centres, it needs to be linked to much harder-edged data analysis about local needs, and effective practice to meet needs. Just doing what parents ask for will not work. But never doing what parents ask for will create a centre that no one wants to use. Giving local people voice needs to be matched with clear negotiation about what data says is needed, particularly for those least likely to be heard. The overarching message here is that engagement is essential, but not sufficient.

The challenges of working across agencies and across government

Both ministers and the NESS team agreed that *joined-up government* working across agencies, professional groups and, indeed, government departments is hard. Fundamentally, organisations and systems have a tendency to see the world through their own prism and there is sometimes an inherent tension between what is good for the organisation and what is effective in achieving the organisation's core purpose. Working together across big bureaucracies will always be extremely difficult. Working together at the front line, where the benefits can be seen on a day-to-day basis, can be easier, not the least because it is so much more dependent on personal relationships among the professionals that need to work together. Moreover, those at the front line are faced with the real needs of families on a day-to-day basis. They are not removed by several layers of management from the problems we are trying to solve through policy. The role of policy is to reduce the barriers that often impede collaboration at the front line. Enshrining in legislation a *duty to cooperate*, as expressed in the Children Act 2004, helps to set an expectation, but it will never ensure the kind of constructive collaboration that is achieved when staff at the front line have shared goals, an understanding and respect for each other's contribution, and, most importantly, line managers who value joint working. Furthermore, as discussed in Chapter Eight, effective inter-agency working is best achieved when staff maintain links with a professional home as well as a collaborative team. A midwife or speech therapist working in a Children's Centre needs to have access to the latest professional training from their health colleagues, and, in so doing, can bring back to health organisations some of the learning from the community base of the Children's Centre.

The critical importance of staff development and improved salary and career structures

A Children's Centre serving a low-income community should be offering a wide range of services, including: evidence-based interventions for particular needs; childcare that not only fits with working patterns, but enriches the social and cognitive development of young children; employment and benefits advice; health and well-being services; and family literacy. The list could be much longer, but the key point is the quality of people delivering the services, and the overall strategy of the centre based on analysis of local need. The quality of the services is largely dependent on the quality of the staff, and the overall strategy and vision is largely dependent on the leadership abilities of the manager. If we want early years services that really do make a difference for children, we need to invest in staff and management development, salaries, and conditions of service. Earlier in this chapter, I identified the failure to understand the scale of the task in running a multi-agency early years centre. We now know much more about how hard the job is; we need to equip staff and managers with the appropriate skills and remuneration to attract the best people.

The need for a performance management system that does not stifle innovation

If we provide the right training and career structure, we still need to know if centres are delivering for local children and families. Building a performance management framework that values and encourages joint working while ensuring that there are clear measures of what is to be achieved, and how to assess different parts of the overall contribution, is another huge challenge. The current government's desire to develop payment-by-results arrangements could very well encourage the thinking that could deliver progress on this difficult task. Most performance regimes are good at ensuring the worst does not happen, but not great at getting the best out of people. New thinking is certainly needed.

The iterative nature of policy development

As described so eloquently by Beverley Hughes, policy development is iterative. As ministers and, indeed, governments change, the learning from policy implementation can be lost. Nationally, as well as locally, policy decisions are based on what politicians believe will be good for the nation. The real success of Sure Start and the wider early years agenda is that politicians and civil servants considered powerful research evidence and evaluation of practice along with value-based beliefs about good outcomes for children. They actively used that evidence to revise the policy as we went along. They held their nerve. Policymaking is a complex process using both evidence, gut views about what is the right thing to do and judgements about what the electorate will accept or even welcome. The danger in policy iteration is that the original purpose can be lost as new thinking emerges. The original purpose of Sure Start was to improve the life chances of *poor* children, the families on the bottom 20% of the income distribution. It was not about the *most disadvantaged* who will be part of that bottom quintile, but only a very small part of it. While most families with entrenched and complex problems are poor, the majority of poor families are not seriously dysfunctional; they just have significantly more challenging circumstances to deal with. We thought we could achieve the goal of improving outcomes for poor children through an area-based initiative. It became clear that by only working in poor areas, we would miss a significant proportion of poor children, those who do not live in disadvantaged areas. Moving from an area-based programme of 500 SSLPs to a universal network of Children's Centres was in part because we learned we would be more successful in reaching the most disadvantaged as well as the wider group of poor families through a universal rather than an area-targeted system. The policy changes were in support of the original goal.

Conclusions

At the time of writing, there continues to be significant support for early years policies and programmes. But key changes are taking place about devolution of control from the centre to local authorities. While the government has announced a new funding stream for *early intervention*, which includes resources for Sure Start Children's Centres, it is not ring-fenced. Authorities under intense pressure are already considering Sure Start to be a soft target. So, the overarching policy goal here seems to be fundamentally about a reduced role for central government in determining local priorities. As Geoff Mulgan points out, relatively young policies need considerable time to bed down. We will be relying on local as well as national politicians to hold their nerve to ensure this relatively recently opened frontier of the welfare state is not dismantled or significantly weakened in the next few years.

The scorecard is three to one. As mentioned earlier in this chapter, we have not succeeded in addressing inequality overall, but have achieved significant success in making the case for universal early years provision and some success in reducing child poverty, an important component of which was the enormous expansion in childcare. Our third success has been the development of a universal network of locally based multi-purpose Children's Centres.

The biggest disappointment is the stubborn nature of social mobility. The most important lesson for me from the last 11 years is the need to address inequality as well as poverty and low attainment. As long as the distance is great between income at the bottom decile and income in the top decile, those of us at the top will always protect the space for our own children. As more and more children do well and get into university, the competition for good jobs will increase. That competition will never be a level playing field because good parents will always share with their children the informal techniques that improve their chances of winning. Ironically, unless there is a huge increase in the number of well-paying jobs, *who you know* will increase rather than decrease in importance because employers are faced with large numbers of degree-level candidates from which to choose. I do not believe efforts to improve health and educational outcomes for children are wasteful of public money. I think they are highly effective for shifting the curve of life chances. They have also greatly improved quality of life: improved health, greatly improved play and leisure facilities, and increased incomes leading to greater access to goods and services. We set out with Sure Start to improve the educational, social and emotional development of young children living in poverty so as to reduce their chances of growing up to be poor as adults. We have probably achieved the first part of that aim, but have been less successful in the second part. Social mobility has largely remained stubbornly static. I believe that without significant redistribution of wealth across social classes, where you are born and who your parents are will remain a significant determinant of life chances. We have tried incredibly hard to reduce the impact. We believe in a fair society, one's attainment should be based on personal effort, not the random chance of who your parents are. We are a long way from that goal. The expectation that early years services, however wonderful, could affect overall inequality was unrealistic. This shift will come from much wider social reforms.

What are the successes, particularly for families with children? Looking back to 1997, I think there are three key successes. First, the importance of services for young children is no longer contested. As in education and health services, there will continue to be debates about what kind of service, delivered by whom, for how long and at what age. There will continue to be debates about maternal employment, maternity and paternity leave, working mothers and fathers. We will continue to argue about targeting and universal services, about home-based or centre-based support, about concentrating on the child or the parent. However, the reality on the ground is a mix of universal and targeted services, some required by central government, others at the behest of local authorities, and some funded through charitable trusts and foundations. The government now accepts the importance of early years, and continues to work to improve provision for the youngest children and continues to emphasise employment as a key route out of poverty.

Second, we have extended the right to a publicly funded early education and childcare service. The public have long supported universal publicly funded education for children aged five and older. They now support the notion of publicly funded early education from the age of three. That service has been made more flexible to suit the needs of working parents, more affordable through childcare tax credits and higher in quality through the Early Years Foundation Stage curriculum. It is not near where it needs to be to make the kind of difference it could make, but the infrastructure is in place.

The third part of the success story is the establishment of Sure Start Children's Centres as the cornerstone of that universal platform, the place where any parent can go for advice and support on a range of child- and sometimes non-child-related issues. The Sure Start brand has proved resilient through good and bad times, but the logo is not important. What is critically important is the ongoing effort to improve outcomes for young children. This can only be done through a platform of universal services that parents are willing to use *and* that can be shown to deliver improved outcomes for children. Unlike school, early years services are not compulsory, but the very high uptake of the service proves their popularity. Within that universal platform, we need a menu of rigorously evaluated, high-quality *interventions* that local commissioners use appropriately.

The fiscal environment in 2011 is very different from 1997, but there are some opportunities to be seized. As was said earlier in this chapter, the movement of services into the voluntary and private sectors may drive new thinking on incentives to drive up quality and reach. But the devil will be in the detail of measurement. The changes to the NHS may also bring opportunities. Can a GP consortium be encouraged to commission services from Children's Centres, bringing a stronger health component into the service mix? The commitment to increase the number of health visitors and to expand the availability of support for teen parents through the Family Nurse Partnership programme could also drive increased collaboration between Children's Centres and health. This may also serve to improve thinking on how to provide the right level of support for all new mothers and babies.

In 1997, we had a patchwork quilt with lots of holes. We still have a quilt, but with almost no gaps and some of the patches are beautiful. The challenge for all public services is to value local diversity while ensuring overall quality. The development of Sure Start provides us with a perfect case study of the advantages, risks and dilemmas inherent in deciding where power should sit. It is a choice between ensuring some form of national equity, which may squeeze out the best, and allowing local control, which may tolerate the worst. Sure Start has by no means solved this problem, but it has taught us much about the issues that need to be considered. It has also proved that government can develop and encourage a new way of working and learn from evidence and experience. Personally, it has been an amazing journey.

Appendix:
Key events and dates

1997   Labour comes to power after 18 years of Conservative government

Establishment of Comprehensive Spending Review (CSR) process

1998   Comprehensive Spending Review on Services for Children under Eight published, Sure Start funding announced in Parliament: total allocation of £450 million over three years, budget £184 million in final year of spending period, 2001/02

1999   January: first Sure Start trailblazer areas announced

March: Prime Minister Tony Blair announces the pledge to end child poverty in a generation and halve child poverty in 10 years

October reshuffle: Tessa Jowell goes to the Department for Education and Employment (DfEE) and Yvette Cooper takes over as Minister for Public Health at the Department of Health (DH) and so takes on responsibility for Sure Start

2000   First CSR after establishment of Sure Start in 1998, programme doubled from 250 local programmes to 500, budget settlement for final year of spending review (2003/04) was £499 million

2001   January: Children and Young People's Unit established at the DfEE to coordinate all policy on children and young people across Whitehall and to administer the Children's Fund

2001   June: general election, creation of the Department for Work and Pensions (DWP) and the Department for Education and Skills (DfES), David Blunkett leaves the DfEE to become Home Secretary; Estelle Morris becomes Secretary of State at the newly created DfES

November: publication of *Tackling Child Poverty* as part of the Pre-Budget Report

2002   May: Hazel Blears replaces Yvette Cooper as Minister for
        Public Health and takes over responsibility for Sure Start,
        reporting to Estelle Morris at the DfES for Sure Start
        matters; Andrew Smith replaces Alistair Darling as Secretary
        of State at the DWP

        July: CSR announcements include the merger of the Sure
        Start Unit with early years and childcare responsibilities at
        the DfES, and joint responsibility for Sure Start moves from
        the DH and DfES to the DWP and DfES

        CSR settlement announced for combined childcare and
        Sure Start Children's Centres, budget for final year of CSR
        period (2005/06) was £1.5 billion

        Baroness Catherine Ashton takes over responsibility for
        Sure Start from Hazel Blears and reports on Sure Start to
        Andrew Smith at the DWP and Estelle Morris at the DfES

        October: Charles Clarke becomes Secretary of State at the
        DfES after resignation of Estelle Morris

2003   Machinery of government changes bring children's social
        care and aspects of family law into the DfES, Margaret
        Hodge becomes the first Children's Minister in overall
        charge of all children's policy including Sure Start, early
        years and childcare, with Baroness Ashton reporting to
        Margaret Hodge on these issues

        Publication of the green paper *Every Child Matters* (ECM),
        creating the framework for a radical restructuring of
        children's services in England

2004   Children Act passed, encompassing most of the
        recommendations in the ECM green paper

        CSR settlement announced for combined childcare and
        Sure Start Children's Centres, £2.27 billion for final year of
        spending period (2007/08)

        September: Baroness Ashton moves to ministerial post at
        Department of Constitutional Affairs; Margaret Hodge takes
        over Ashton's early years' responsibilities

        December: publication of *Choice for Parents, the Best Start for
        Children: A Ten Year Childcare Strategy*

December: Charles Clarke becomes Home Secretary and is replaced at the DfES by Ruth Kelly

2005   After the election, Margaret Hodge moves to the Department of Culture, Media and Sport, being replaced as Children's Minister by Beverley Hughes; David Blunkett takes over from Andrew Smith as Secretary of State at the DWP

2006   Ruth Kelly resigns, replaced as Secretary of State at the DfES by Alan Johnson

Childcare Act passed, encompassing many of the commitments in the 2004 Ten Year Strategy on childcare

2009   Apprenticeships, Skills, Children and Learning Act passed, making the provision of Children's Centres a statutory requirement for local authorities

Celebration marking 3,000 Children's Centres opened

2010   March: just over 3,500 Children's Centres operating, as promised in the 2004 Childcare Strategy

May: general election, Conservative–Liberal Democrat Coalition government formed with renewed interest in early intervention, families with complex problems and commitment to Sure Start Children's Centres

References

Allen, G. (2011) *Early Intervention, the Next Steps*. London: HMG.

Anning, A. and National Evaluation of Sure Start Team (2007) *National Evaluation Summary, Understanding Variations in Effectiveness amongst Sure Start Local Programmes: Lessons for Sure Start Children's Centres*. Nottingham: DfES Publications.

Anning, A., Stuart, J., Nicholls, M., Godthorpe, J. and Morley, A. (2007) *National Evaluation Report: Understanding Variations in Effectiveness amongst Sure Start Local Programmes*. Nottingham: DfES publications.

Barber, M. (2007) *Instructions to Deliver Fighting to Transform Britain's Public Services*. London: Methuen.

Barnes, J. (2007) 'Targeting deprived areas: the nature of the Sure Start Local Programme neighbourhoods', in J. Belsky, J. Barnes and E. Melhuish (eds) *The National Evaluation of Sure Start: Does Area-Based Early Intervention Work?* Bristol: The Policy Press.

Barnes, J., Broomfield, K., Frost, M., Harper, G., McLeod, A., Knowles, J. and Leyland, A. (2003) *Sure Start National Evaluation Summary, Characteristics of Sure Start Local Programme Areas: Rounds 1–4*. Nottingham: DfES.

Barnes, J., Cheng, H., Howden, B., Frost, M., Harper, G., Lattin-Rawstrone, R., Sak, C. and the Ness Team (2007) *National Evaluation Summary: Changes in the Characteristics of SSLP Areas between 2000/01 and 2004/05*. Nottingham: DfES Publications.

Barnett, W.S. (1996) *Lives in the Balance: Age 27 Benefit–Cost Analysis of the High/Scope Perry Preschool Program*, monographs of the High/Scope Educational Research Foundation no 11. Ypsilanti, MI: High Scope Press.

Belsky, J. and Melhuish, E. (2007) 'Impact of Sure Start Local Programmes on Children and Families', in J. Belsky, J. Barnes and E. Melhuish (eds) *The National Evaluation of Sure Start: Does Area-Based Early Intervention Work*. Bristol: The Policy Press, pp 133–53.

Belsky, J., Melhuish, E., Barnes, J., Leyland, A., Romaniuk, H. and the NESS Team (2007) 'Effects of Sure Start Local Programmes on children and families: early findings from a quasi-experimental, cross sectional study', *British Medical Journal*. Available at: www.bmj.com/cgi/content/full/332/7556/1476

Bennett, R. (2006) 'Poor turned off Sure Start by middle class mothers', *The Times*, 6 October.

Bruner, J. (1980) *Under Five in Britain*. London: Grant McIntyre.

Bynner, J., Ferri, E., Plewis, I., Kelly, Y., Marmot, M., Pickering, K., Smith, T. and Smith, G. (1999) 'Sure Start evaluation development project, report to the Sure Start Unit', unpublished report.

Cabinet Office (1999) 'Guide to the centre of government part III: the modernisation agenda'. Available at: http://webarchive. nationalarchives.gov.uk/20100807034701/http://archive. cabinetoffice.gov.uk/roleofcentre/modagenda.htm#reform

Carneiro, P. and Heckman, J. (2003) 'Human capital policy', in J. Heckman, A. Krueger and B. Friedman (eds) *Inequality in America: What Role for Human Capital Policies?* Cambridge: MIT Press.

CYPU (Children and Young People's Unit) (2001a) *Tomorrow's Future: Building a Strategy for Children and Young People.* London: DfEE Children and Young People's Unit.

CYPU (2001b) *Building a Strategy for Children and Young People.* London: DfEE Children and Young People's Unit.

Conservative Party (2001) *Time for Common Sense.* London: Conservative Party.

Curnow, N. (2006) 'Sure Start workers rebut criticisms', 22 September. Available at: www.nurseryworld.co.uk/news/719852/Sure-Start-workers-rebut-criticisms/DCMP

DCSF (Department for Children, Schools and Families) (2009) *Next Steps for Early Learning and Childcare: Building on the 10-year Strategy.* Nottingham: DCSF Publications.

Dean, M. (1999) 'Bringing up parents; are we nearly there yet? Unhappily not', *The Guardian*, 27 December.

Denny, C. (2000) 'Children in the poorest families get help to succeed at school,' *The Guardian*, 19 July.

DfEE (Department for Education and Employment) (1999) *Sure Start, Making a Difference for Children and Families.* Sudbury: DfEE Publications.

DfEE (2000) *Sure Start National Evaluation: Specification of Requirements – June 2000.*

DfES (2002) 'Sure Start', 11 December. Nottingham: DfES Publications..

Dorling, D. (2010) *Injustice: Why Social Inequality Persists.* Bristol: The Policy Press.

Eisenstadt, N. (1983) 'Working with families and the community: a study of two family centres', unpublished MSc thesis, Cranfield Institute of Technology.

Eisenstadt, N. (2005) 'Director defends "influential" Sure Start', *The Guardian*, Children's Services Supplement, 15 February, pp 257-64.

Field, F. (2010) *The Foundation Years: Preventing Poor Children from Becoming Poor Adults.* London: HMG.

Glass, N. (1999) 'Sure Start: the development of an early intervention programme for young children in the United Kingdom', *Children and Society*, vol 13, pp 257-64.

Glass, N. (2005) 'Surely some mistake', *The Guardian*, 5 January. Available at: www.guardian.co.uk/society/2005/jan/05/guardiansocietysupplement.childrensservices

HMG (Her Majesty's Government) (2002) *Inter Departmental Childcare Review: Delivering for Children and Families*. Norwich: HMSO.

HMG (2003) *Every Child Matters*. Norwich: The Stationery Office.

HMSO (Her Majesty's Stationery Office) (1999) *Modernising Government*. HMSO.

HMT (Her Majesty's Treasury) (1998) *Public Services for the Future: Modernisation, Reform, Accountability*, Chapter 26, 'Sure Start (Interim PSA)'. HMSO.

HMT (1998) *Modern Public Services for Britain: Investing in Reform*, 'Chapter 21, Cross Departmental Review of Services for Young Children'. London: The Stationery Office.

HMT (1999) *Public Services for the Future: Modernisation, Reform, Accountability, Comprehensive Spending Review 1999–2002 March 1999 Supplement*. HMSO.

HMT (2000) *2000 Spending Review, Public Service Agreements*, White Paper, Chapter 20, Sure Start. http://archive.treasury.gov.uk/sr2000/psa/4808-20.html

HMT (2001) *Tackling Child Poverty: Giving Every Child the Best Possible Start in Life*. London: HM Tresury.

HMT (2002) *2002 Spending Review, Public Service Agreements*. The Stationery Office.

HMT (2004) *Choice for Parents, the Best Start for Children: A Ten Year Strategy for Childcare*. Norwich: HMSO.

House of Commons, Children, Schools and Families Committee (2009) 'Sure Start children's centres', 9 November. London: The Stationery Office.

Labour Party (2001) *Ambitions for Britain: Labour's Manifesto 2001*. Sutton: HH Associates.

Marmot, M. (2010) *Fair Society, Healthy Lives: The Marmot Review Strategy Review [sense?] of Health Inequalities in England post 2010*. London: the Marmot Review.

Meadows, P. (2006) *Cost Effectiveness of Implementing SSLPs: an Interim Report*. Nottingham: DfES.

Meadows, P. (2007) 'The costs and benefits of Sure Start Local Programmes', in J. Belsky, J. Barnes and E. Melhuish (eds) *The National Evaluation of Sure Start: Does Area-Based Early Intervention Work*. Bristol: The Policy Press.

Meadows, P. and Garbers, C. (2004) *Improving the Employability of Parents in Sure Start Programmes*, National Evaluation Summary. **[place?]** DfES Publications.

Melhuish, E. and Hall, D. (2007) 'The policy background to Sure Start', in J. Belsky, J. Barnes and E. Melhuish (eds) *The National Evaluation of Sure Start: Does Area-Based Early Intervention Work*. Bristol: The Policy Press.

Melhuish, E.C. and National Evaluation of Sure Start Team (2002) 'Asking the right questions: the national evaluation of Sure Start', *Interplay*, no 1, pp 26–31.

Melhuish, E.C., Belsky, J., Anning, A., Ball, M., Barnes, J., Romaniuk, H., Leyland, A. and NESS Research Team (2007) 'Variation in Sure Start Local Programme implementation and its consequences for children and families', *Journal of child Psychology and Psychiatry*, no 48, pp 543–51.

Melhuish, E., Belsky, J., Leyland, A., Barnes, J. and National Evaluation of Sure Start Research Team (2008a) 'Effects of fully-established Sure Start Local Programmes on 3-year-old children and their families living in England: a quasi-experimental observational study', *The Lancet*, vol 372, pp 1641–7.

Melhuish, E., Sylva, K., Sammons, P., Siraj-Blatchford, I., Taggart, B., Phan, M. and Malin, A. (2008b) 'Preschool influences on mathematics achievement', *Science*, vol 321, no 5893, pp 1161–2.

Melhuish, E., Belsky, J., MacPherson, K. and Cullis, A. (2010) *The Quality of Group Childcare Settings Used by 3–4 Year Old Children in Sure Start Local Programme Areas, and the Relationship with Child Outcomes*. Nottingham: DfE publications.

Mintzberg, H. and Quinn, J. (1996) *The Strategy Process*. New Jersey: Prentice Hall International.

Munro, E. (2010) *Munro Review of Child Protection, Part One: A Systems Analysis*. DfE.

Munro, E. (2011) *Munro Review of Child Protection, Interim Report: the Child's Journey*. DfE.

National Evaluation of Sure Start Research Team (2005) *Early Impacts of Sure Start Local Programmes on Children and Families*, Sure Start Report 13. London: DfES.

National Evaluation of Sure Start Research Team (2008) *The Impact of Sure Start Local Programmes on Three Year Olds and Their Families*, Sure Start Report 27. London: HMSO.

National Evaluation of Sure Start Team (2010) *The Impact of Sure Start Local Programmes on Child Development and Family Functioning: Report of the Longitudinal Study of 5-year-old Children and their Families*. London: DfE.

Olds, D., Kitzman, H., Cole, R., Robinson, J., Sidora, K., Luckey, D., Henderson, R., Hanks, C., Bondy, J. and Holmberg, J. (2004) 'Effects of nurse home-visiting on maternal life course and child development: age 6 follow up results of a randomized trial', *Pediatrics*, vol 114, no 6, pp 1550–9.

Public Audit Forum (1999) *Implications for Audit of the Modernising Government Agenda*. www.public-audit-forum.gov.uk/pafmodgov.pdf

Pugh, G. (1996) 'A policy for early childhood services', in G. Pugh (ed) *Contemporary Issues in the Early Years*. London: Paul Chapman and National Children's Bureau.

Rutter, M. (2007) 'Sure Start Local Programmes: an outsider's perspective', in J. Belsky, J. Barnes and E. Melhuish (eds) *The National Evaluation of Sure Start: Does Area-Based Early Intervention Work*. Bristol: The Policy Press.

Sammons, P. (2010) 'Does pre-school make a difference?', in K. Sylva, E. Melhuish, P. Sammons, I. Siraj-Blatchford and B. Taggart (eds) *Early Childhood Matters: Evidence from the Effective Pre-School and Primary Education Project*. London: Routledge.

Schweinhart, L. and Weikart, D. (1993) *The High/Scope Perry Preschool Study Through Age 27*. Ypsilanti: High/Scope Press.

Sefton, T., Hills, J. and Sutherland, H. (2009) 'Poverty, inequality, and redistribution', in J. Hills, T. Sefton and K. Stewart (eds) *Towards a More Equal Society*. Bristol: The Policy Press.

Siraj-Blatchford, I. and Siraj-Blatchford, J. (2009) *Improving Development Outcomes for Children through Effective Practice in Integrating Early Years Services*. London: Centre for Excellence in Outcomes in Children's and Young People's Services.

Smith, A. and May, H. (2006) 'Early childhood care and education in Aotearoa-New Zealand', in E. Melhuish and K. Petrogiannins (eds) *Early Childhood Care and Education: International Perspectives*. London: Routledge.

Smith, M.K. (2004, 2005) 'Extended schooling – some issues for informal and community education', *The Encyclopedia of Informal Education*. Available at: www.infed.org/schooling/extended_schooling.htm. [Note: this article uses some material from Smith, M.K. (2000, 2004) 'Full-service schooling', *The Encyclopedia of Informal Education*, www.infed.org/schooling/f-serv.htm]

Social Exclusion Unit (1998) *Truancy and School Exclusion*. London: The Stationery Office.

Sylva, K. (2010a) 'Quality in early childhood settings', in K. Sylva, E. Melhuish, P. Sammons, I. Siraj-Blatchford and B. Taggart (eds) *Early Childhood Matters: Evidence from the Effective Pre-School and Primary Education Project*. London: Routledge.

Sylva, K. (2010b) 'Rethinking the evidence base for early years policy and practice', in K. Sylva, E. Melhuish, P. Sammons, I. Siraj-Blatchford and B. Taggart (eds) *Early Childhood Matters: Evidence from the Effective Pre-School and Primary Education Project*. London: Routledge.

Sylva, K., Melhuish, E., Sammons, P., Siraj-Blatchford, I. and Taggart, B. (eds) (2010) *Early Childhood Matters: Evidence from the Effective Pre-School and Primary Education Project*. London: Routledge.

Taggart, B. (2010) 'Making a difference: how research can inform policy', K. Sylva, E. Melhuish, P. Sammons, I. Siraj-Blatchford and B. Taggart (eds) *Early Childhood Matters: Evidence from the Effective Pre-School and Primary Education Project*. London: Routledge.

Tunstill, J., Allnock, D., Meadows, P. and McCleod, A. (2002) *Sure Start National Evaluation: Early Experiences of Implementing Sure Start*. Nottingham: DfES Publications.

Waldfogel, J. (1997) 'The new wave of service integration', *Social Services Review*, vol 71, no 3, pp 467–8.

Waldfogel, J. (2006) *What Children Need*. Cambridge: Harvard University Press.

Waldfogel, J. (2010) *Britain's War on Poverty*. New York: Russell Sage Foundation.

Wilkinson, R. and Pickett, K. (2010) *The Spirit Level: Why Equality is Better for Everyone*. London: Penguin Books.

Wintour, P. (2006) 'Blair admits failing most needy children', *The Guardian*, 16 May.

Index

Note: The following abbreviations have been used: t = table; f = figure.